Box Turtle Pet Owner's Guide.

The Captive Care of Box Turtles.

Including Box Turtles Biology, Behavior and
Ecology.

I0173705

by

Ben Team

Published by: IMB Publishing

Table of Contents

About the Author

Ben Team is an environmental educator and author with over 16 years of professional reptile-keeping experience.

Ben currently maintains www.FootstepsInTheForest.com, where he shares information, narration and observations of the natural world. When not writing about plants, animals and habitats, Ben enjoys spending time with his beautiful wife.

Foreword

To children across much of North America, box turtles are called such because you can find them crossing the road, and take them home and put them in a box.

After placing the turtle in the box, you add a repurposed margarine tub as a water dish (which the turtle will undoubtedly tip over), a handful of sticks and leaves (so he doesn't realize he has been removed from the forest) and a few leaves of lettuce for food (which the box turtle almost never eats).

Not surprisingly, the turtle fails to thrive in this type of environment. Within two days of staring at your new pet -- who remains in its shell more-or-less constantly -- you liberate the turtle and the box that served as his home.

These types of encounters occur every day, and, while they are unlikely to be fun for the reptiles, they undoubtedly foster an appreciation for nature among the world's youngest inhabitants.

Provided that the turtle is released in the same place where he or she was found, spending a day or two in a human home is unlikely to cause serious problems.

This is important, as box turtle populations are declining in most parts of their range, thanks to habitat destruction and over collection for the pet trade.

While box turtles make excellent pets, they have a number of important husbandry requirements, which must be met if they are to remain healthy. Unfortunately, providing the proper care for a box turtle is beyond the capabilities of most young children.

However, adults and older children can often provide a great home for a box turtle, particularly if the turtle is a captive bred animal.

In such cases, the human and animal both benefit from the relationship. The human gets to enjoy a little slice of nature, while the turtle enjoys an existence characterized by unlimited food, protection from predators and veterinary care in the case of illness or injury.

***

Box turtles are unusual turtles, whose shells possess a hinge. This hinge allows the turtle to seal the borders around the margin of the shell, once it has withdrawn its head and legs inside. This provides them with greater protection than most other turtles enjoy.

In fact, it is the ability of box turtles to close their shell – as one may close a box – that has given rise to the animals' common name.

These hinge-shelled turtles are also unusual in another way: Unlike the vast majority of other turtle species with whom they share their natural range (most of whom are aquatic), box turtles spend most of their time on dry ground. This leads many to label them as tortoises, but this term is better reserved for the true tortoises of the world.

Aside from these unusual characteristics, box turtles exhibit relatively normal biology, natural history and behavior by turtle standards. They live long, slow lives and subsist on

food that is easy for these lumbering reptiles to catch –
primarily vegetation, fungus and invertebrates.

Although the young are at risk to a variety of predators, the
adults are rather safe. Aside from the odd canid or human,
adult box turtles rarely end up on another animal's menu.
While humans undoubtedly consumed more than a few box
turtles throughout history, habitat destruction and
collection for the pet trade are more common threats in the
modern era.

***

If you elect to maintain a captive box turtle or two, make
sure that you understand – and are equipped to provide for
– your turtle's needs. This includes being prepared to care
for a pet whose lifespan is measured in decades.

Additionally, if you wish to acquire a pet box turtle, always
select captive bred animals. Not only do captive bred
animals adapt better to captivity, they do not represent a
drain on wild populations.

PART I: BOX TURTLES

Properly caring for any animal requires an understanding of the species and its place in the natural world. This includes subjects as disparate as anatomy and ecology, diet and geography, and reproduction and physiology.

It is only by learning what your pet is, how it lives, what it does that you can achieve the primary goal of animal husbandry: Providing your pet with the highest quality of life possible.

Chapter 1: Box Turtle Description and Anatomy

Although their shells possess unique adaptations, box turtles have the same basic morphology as most other terrestrial or semi-terrestrial chelonians.

Box turtles possess a typical, bilaterally symmetric vertebrate body plan, including a head, long neck, tail, four legs and a large shell.

Size

Box turtles are relatively small chelonians. Hatchlings are measure about 1 to 1 ½ inches (2.54 to 3.81 centimeters) long and weigh about one-fifth to one-quarter ounce (5 to 7 grams) when they emerge from their eggs.

Most adult box turtles measure between 4 and 6 inches (10 to 15 centimeters) in length and weigh about 1 to 2 pounds (450 to 900 grams). However, rare individuals may reach or exceed 8 inches (20 centimeters) in length.

Color and Pattern

The colors and markings of box turtles are highly variable. Different species and subspecies have different characteristic color patterns, but individuals also exhibit a great deal of individual variation.

Box turtle shells typically have a brown, black, gray or tan ground color, which is often covered with lighter markings. These markings, which are usually yellow, cream or orange, may take the form of blotches, stripes or spots.

Alternatively, some subspecies tend to be uniformly colored animals with no obvious markings.

The skin of a box turtle's legs, neck and tail may be nearly black, brown, khaki or straw-colored, and it may feature lighter colored dots or markings.

Some box turtles exhibit sexually dimorphic colors. For example, male ornate box turtles (*Terrapene ornata ornata*) typically have yellow to green heads, while females have essentially brown heads.

Occasional specimens display abnormal pigmentation.

Shell

Box turtles have rigid, domed shells, which provide them with protection from predators. When viewed from above, the shells are oval in shape.

Box turtle shells are sexually dimorphic, meaning that males and females have shells of slightly different shapes. The shells of females are more highly domed than the shells of males. Additionally, while females have essentially flat plastrons, males have concave plastrons. This concave shape allows the males to mount the females while mating.

These shells are created from a combination of rib bones and dermal plates (bony plates that originate within the skin). Keratinized plates, called scutes, lie on top of the bony layer.

Interestingly, the plate-like bones outnumber the keratin-based scutes. This means that the margins of the scutes do not occur in the same places that the bones fuse together, which gives additional strength to the shell.

The top portion of a box turtle's shell is called the carapace, the bottom portion is called the plastron and the portion of the shell that connects the carapace to the plastron is called the lateral bridge.

Box turtles have five vertebral (or central) scutes that form a row down the center of the back. Flanking the vertebral scutes are the costal (or pleural) scutes, numbering eight in total (four on each side).

Twenty-two marginal scutes lie around the margin of the carapace (11 on each side), and a pair of supracaudal scutes sit right above the turtle's tail. Box turtles have a small nuchal scute located directly above a turtle's head and neck along the anterior margin of the carapace.

The plastron features six pairs of scutes, termed (moving posteriorly) the gulars, humerals, pectorals, abdominals, femorals and anals.

A flexible hinge lies across the plastron, between the abdominal and pectoral scutes. This hinge allows box turtles to close their shells. This offers an even greater degree of protection than most other turtles enjoy – the legs, face and tails of most other turtles remain exposed after being pulled into the shell.

Hatchling box turtles have relatively soft, flexible shells. The shell will harden over time, but they remain especially vulnerable to predators until then.

Turtles are firmly attached to their shells; they cannot crawl out of them, as is frequently seen in cartoons and comic strips. Accordingly, a turtle's shell grows along with the turtle.

An eastern box turtle, peering out of a partially closed shell.

The periodic nature of this phenomenon (the shells grow quickly during the active season and cease growing in the winter) causes growth rings to form on the scutes. You can arrive at a reasonable estimation of a box turtle's age by counting these rings. However, a variety of factors can cause these rings to indicate incorrect ages.

Some individuals may produce more than one growth ring per year; while other turtles live in areas with very long growing seasons and short (or absent) dormant seasons, which disrupts the annual nature of the process.

Additionally, the shells of many turtles – particularly mature specimens – often show signs of wear. If this wear occurs near the growth rings, some of the rings may be obscured.

Legs

Box turtles have strong, muscular legs that allow them to move throughout their habitat. Their pillar-like legs are covered in broad, overlapping scales. Despite their relative comfort in shallow water, box turtles lack webbing on their feet.

Most box turtles have five toes on their front feet, and four toes on their rear feet. However, the aptly named three-toed box turtle (*Terrapene carolina triunguis*) usually bears three toes on the rear feet. Occasionally, individuals that appear like three-toed box turtles have rear feet with four toes; it is not yet clear whether this is a result of integration with eastern box turtles (*Terrapene carolina carolina*) or developmental anomalies.

The claws on the rear feet of male box turtles are strongly hooked, which may provide them with a tool for prying open the rear portion of a female's shell when they are attempting to mate.

Head, Neck and Face

Like all other living turtles, box turtles lack teeth. Instead, they have a bony beak (technically called a rhamphotheca), which is covered by a layer of keratin. Their beaks have evolved a sharp, cutting edge that helps them slice food into smaller pieces. The dorsal half of the beak is often strongly hooked. The tongue is fleshy, muscular and used to manipulate food in the mouth.

The eyes of box turtles sit on the sides of their heads, although the front of their faces are slightly constricted, which allows them to see in front of their face as well as to the sides. Their nostrils lie on the front of their faces, directly in front of their eyes.

The only portion of the box turtle's ear that is visible is the tympanum (eardrum), which sits just behind the bottom jaw.

Tail

Box turtles have relatively short tails. The tails play little to no role in locomotion or defense, but they do serve as the location for the vent, which is important in elimination and reproduction.

Although immature males and females have similar-looking tails, those of mature males are longer and thicker than those of mature females are. Additionally, the location of the vent on the tail differs in males and females. In females, the vent is located inside the margin of the shell; the vents of males are located more distally, and they lie outside the margin of the vent. This arrangement allows males to breed with the females.

Internal Anatomy

While the average turtle keeper need not understand the internal anatomy of their pet enough to perform exploratory surgery, a basic understanding of the turtle's internal world is necessary.

In most respects, turtles have internal anatomy that is similar to that of other vertebrates, such as humans. Accordingly, special attention is warranted for those aspects that differ from those of most other animals.

Skeletal System

One of the unique aspects of the internal anatomy of turtles is their skeletal system.

As with most other vertebrates, turtles have both axial and appendicular skeletons. The skull, vertebral column and ribs form the axial skeleton, while the shoulder girdle, pelvic girdle and limbs comprise the appendicular skeleton.

However, in turtles, the ribs are fused to the shell. Unlike other vertebrates, whose pelvic and hip girdles are located *outside* the rib cage, turtles carry these bones *inside* their rib cage. While this arrangement helps to protect these areas from damage, it limits the mobility of most turtles.

Digestive System

The digestive system of box turtles is similar to that of other turtles, and, to a lesser extent, vertebrates in general.

Just inside the mouth likes the esophagus, which transports food to the stomach. From here, food passes through the small and then large intestines before being expelled from the vent.

The pancreas and spleen lie close to the stomach, while the gallbladder attaches to the liver, just as it does in most other vertebrates.

Circulatory and Pulmonary System

In general, the circulatory and pulmonary systems of turtles are similar to those of other reptiles.

Turtles inhale and exhale through their mouth or nose, while the trachea carries air to and from two lungs. Because the turtle's shell is rigid, which prevents the ribs from moving (which would pump air into and out of the lungs), turtles have a collection of membranes and connective tissues that attach to the distal ends of the lungs. When these connective tissues contract and relax, the lungs empty and fill with air.

Like many other reptiles, turtles have three-chambered hearts, which feature two atria and a single ventricle. One atrium accepts oxygenated blood from the lungs, while the other atrium receives oxygen-poor blood from the body.

Both atria pump blood into a single ventricle, which then pumps the blood into the rest of the body. Normally, as in many other reptiles, this means that the turtle's body receives a combination of oxygen-rich and oxygen-poor blood. However, turtles have a primitive septum (wall) in their ventricle, which partially prevents the mixing of the two types of blood.

Accordingly, turtles have a slightly more efficient cardiovascular system than lizards and snakes do.

Urinary System
Box turtles filter waste products from their bloodstream via their paired kidneys. They then store these waste products in the urinary bladder. These waste products are released in the form of urea (they are ureotelic). (Wallace B Baze, 1970)

Turtles have a renal portal blood system, which means that the blood traveling through the rear half of the turtles' body is filtered by the kidneys before making it to the front half of the body. This has important implications in turtle medical care; medications cannot be injected into the rear half of the body, as they kidneys will filter the medications before they can circulate widely.

Reproductive System

Turtle fertilization occurs internally, so they must mate to reproduce.

Males have a single intromittent organ (penis), making them similar to crocodilians and birds, but very different from snakes and lizards, who possess paired reproductive organs (termed hemipenes).

The penis of male box turtles is held inverted, inside the tail base. During mating attempts, the penis everts and protrudes outside of the vent.

Females have a pair of ovaries, in which eggs form and reside; and a pair of oviducts, which accept the eggs once they are released. The eggs join the sperm inside the oviducts, where they continue to develop.

Before the eggs are deposited, calcium and other minerals coat the surface of the developing embryos, thus giving rise to the eggshell.

Like females of many other species, box turtles can retain sperm from a single mating for at least 14 months. (Gist, 1975)

Chapter 2: Box Turtle Biology and Behavior

Box turtles exhibit a number of biological and behavioral adaptations that allow them to survive in their natural habitats.

Growth

The growth rate of box turtles varies widely from one species and specimen to the next, as well as in relation to the amount of food they can acquire. Wild box turtles may fail to grow for several years if they are unable to obtain sufficient food.

Box turtles probably grow more quickly in captivity than they do in the wild, but occasional captives appear to grow very slowly.

In the broadest terms, your 1-inch-long hatchling may approach 2 inches (5 centimeters) in length by its first birthday. Over the next several years, the turtle will continue to grow, albeit at a slower rate.

If provided with ideal husbandry, box turtles can reach about half of their adult size – 2- to 3-inches in length and 250 grams in weight – by their second birthday.

By 5 or 6 years of age, most captive box turtles are approaching maturity, and have reached lengths between 4 and 5 inches (10 and 12 centimeters) in size. Wild box turtles likely require at least twice this length of time to reach maturity. Those living in northern latitudes (who must contend with a short growing season) may take four times as long to reach maturity.

Shedding

Like all other animals, box turtles shed their skin; however, unlike snakes and lizards, who shed all of their scales at the same time, box turtles shed on a rather continual basis. Because they replace very small pieces of skin at a time, the process is not terribly obvious.

However, at some times – particularly during periods of rapid growth – box turtles may increase the amount of skin they shed in a short time period, which makes the process more conspicuous. Your pet may ingest his shed skin in an effort to avoid wasting any nutrients.

Occasionally, box turtles suffer from injuries or illnesses that cause them to shed abnormally.

Box turtles do not shed their scutes; instead, new material is added to the scutes during phases of rapid growth. The same scutes that adorn the top of a hatchling's carapace will be there for his or her 50th birthday, should he or she live that long.

Lifespan

Most turtles live long lives, and box turtles are no exception. As is the case for most other chelonians, most mortality likely occurs among eggs, hatchlings and juveniles, rather than mature adults. However, things like wildfires, disease and road mortality remain significant threats for the entirety of the turtles' lives.

Most box turtles that reach maturity likely live for about 30 to 40 years of age. However, many live much longer than this.

A 2001 study by J.K. Miller documented several gravid females, thought to be 60 years old or older. (Miller, 2001)

Several accounts of 100-year-old box turtles exist. However, few – if any – have the provenance to prove their age. Nevertheless, few scientists dispute the presumed fact that box turtles can live for a century or longer.

Senses and Intelligence

Box turtles possess the same senses that most other turtles do. They have reasonably good eyesight, respond to tactile stimulation readily and appear to have a strong sense of smell. However, box turtle hearing is average at best.

Turtles have a larger brain size index than most lizards and snakes do, but this does not mean they are especially intelligent. Nevertheless, many box turtles learn to anticipate routine maintenance, and they may even begin to associate their keeper with food. This can lead them to "beg" for food, by repeatedly crawling toward you as you approach.

Metabolism and Digestion

Like most other non-avian reptiles, box turtles have slow metabolisms. This not only means that it takes them longer than many other animals to process their food, but also, they require less food to remain alive. In general, ectothermic ("cold-blooded") animals require about one-fifth to one-twentieth of the food that similarly sized endothermic ("warm-blooded") animal do.

Box turtles typically feed heavily throughout the spring, summer and fall, so that they can fast during brumation (the reptilian equivalent of hibernation).

Locomotion

Despite their bulky build and ungainly appearance, box are capable of traveling long distances. Their strong, thick legs provide a stable base of support and their sense of balance keeps them from tipping over while walking.

If you watch a box turtle walk, you will usually see it move its legs in an alternating pattern. First, it swings the rear right leg and front left leg (for instance) forward, then, upon gaining purchase, it swings the other two legs forward. The front leg usually lands slightly before the rear leg does.

Of course, the animals adjust these movement patterns to negotiate uneven terrain or objects, so not all steps take on this pattern. The head helps to maintain balance during locomotion, while the tail plays essentially no role.

Although they would never be considered good climbers, box turtles often surprise their owners with their ability to scale obstacles.

Diel Behavioral Patterns

Box turtles are primarily diurnal animals, meaning that they are active during the day and sleep during the night. However, they adjust their activity patterns to take advantage of the most advantageous temperatures and humidity.

For example, while box turtles are most likely to be active during mid-day when the temperatures are cool and the sun shining, while they are most active during the early morning and late evening during the height of the summer, when ambient temperatures are too high.

In captivity, where they are provided with nearly ideal climates, they may be active at any hour of the day or night. Nevertheless, actual nocturnal activity is relatively rare.

Seasonal Behavioral Patterns

Box turtle seasonal patterns vary greatly from one taxa or location to the next. Subspecies living in grassy, continental habitats usually hibernate during the cold, long winters. Conversely, those living in tropical regions usually remain active all year long. Some may even become semi-dormant during prolonged heatwaves.

Generally speaking, the duration of the active season decreases as latitude increases.

Box turtles will move toward more mesic (wet) habitats during prolonged warm, dry weather. Conversely, they often become very active and more likely to travel long distances immediately after rains.

Defensive Strategies

Box turtles try to lead a low-profile lifestyle, and avoid encounters with predators whenever possible. Their cryptic colors and patterns help to accomplish this goal, as does their habit of using subterranean retreats and debris piles to remain hidden from view.

When confronted with a predator, box turtles withdraw their heads into their shells and draw the opening of the shells closed. This helps to provide their legs, tail and face with additional protection. They will often remain in this position for a considerable period of time, until they are sure the danger has passed.

Mature box turtles occasionally fall prey to raccoons, canids and felids, but they are generally safe from most common predators. (William R. Belzer, 2000) In fact, once a turtle has reached about 250 grams in weight, they are as safe as they will be once they reach a mature weight of 500 grams.

Hatchling and juvenile box turtles, on the other hand, are vulnerable to a wide variety of predators in their natural habitats. Some of their predators include birds, raccoons, opossums, rats, chipmunks, squirrels, snakes, and large lizards.

Note the plastral hinge on the right side of the photo.

Accordingly, small box turtles usually try to remain hidden (or at least inconspicuous) as much as possible, in order to avoid attracting the attention of predators.

Foraging

Box turtles are opportunistic generalists, who consume a wide variety of foods. They eat both plants and animals, although the relative proportion of one to the other changes over the course of their lives. Hatchlings and juveniles primarily consume animals, while adults incorporate much more vegetable matter in their diets.

Box turtles tend to forage actively, although they will quickly pounce on food items that appear suddenly. Many people are stunned to discover the quickness with which a motivated box turtle can move when pursuing food.

Although it remains to be conclusively demonstrated, box turtles appear to be quite aware of where food sources are located within their territory.

Breeding Behavior

Male and female box turtles often inhabit overlapping or adjacent territories, so neither gender undertakes long mate-searching treks. Instead, it is likely that males mate with females whenever they are encountered, as long as temperatures permit activity.

After mounting a female, a male box turtle will try to insert the inner claws of his rear legs inside the shell of the female. Presumably, this helps him to keep the rear portion of the shell open, and allow mating.

Males often bite at the heads of females during mating. Although they rarely make contact, it can look quite violent to human observers. Males often exhibit breeding behavior when they encounter other males, including mounting, engaging the rear claws and biting at the head of the other male. (Stickel, 1989)

Adults begin courting and breeding in the late spring, with egg deposition occurring during mid- to late-summer. Eggs hatch from late summer to early fall. Hatchlings in some locations remain in the nest for their first fall and winter, and emerge in the spring.

Females can store sperm for several years, which allows them to deposit eggs for several years after an initial mating. Once it is time to deposit the eggs, females often travel very long distances to find nesting locations. Preferred sites usually feature a sandy substrate and ample insolation.

Females will dig their nests several inches deep and cover them thoroughly after depositing the clutch. Most clutches contain between two and eight eggs. The females will have no contact with the young (except through happenstance) after this point.

Chapter 3: Box Turtle Taxonomy and Phylogeny

Although terrestrial turtles are often adorned with the "tortoise" moniker, it is not appropriate for box turtles.

The term "tortoise" is best applied to turtles of the family Testudinidae, rather than to turtles who live terrestrial lifestyles. While it is true most terrestrial chelonians belong to this family, box turtles represent a distinct lineage, nestled within the same group as many of the other "freshwater" turtles that live within their range.

Additionally, box turtles are much more aquatic than many other "terrestrial" turtles. Most will spend some time in the water, and one species of box turtle is essentially aquatic.

But before delving more deeply into the classification and familial relationships among box turtles, it is helpful to begin with a broader context.

Reptiles in the Tree of Life

For decades, scientists have debated the definition of the term "reptile." (Anderson, 2003)

On the one hand, lizards, snakes, crocodiles and turtles are all instantly recognizable as reptiles, thanks to their scaly skin and other traits.

However, the reptile evolutionary lineage, when considered in its entirety, must also include dinosaurs, and their direct descendants, the birds.

Regardless of which definition taxonomists ultimately agree upon, the history of the group is relatively well known. Reptiles first evolved approximately 300 million years ago, when they branched off the amphibian family tree.

This lineage produced an amazing array of species, including dinosaurs, mosasaurs and pterodactyls, as well as the ancestors of modern snakes, lizards and turtles. Most of these lineages died out almost completely, but a few managed to survive to the present day. Currently, reptiles are represented by the following groups:

- Crocodilians
- Squamates (snakes and lizards)
- Sphenodontids (tuataras)
- Testudines (turtles)
- Birds

Testudines in the Tree of Life

All living turtles can trace their origin back to the same ancestral species, meaning that all living turtles are part of the same evolutionary lineage. Scientists call such groups monophyletic.

Two different names are commonly used to refer to the group, including "testudines" and "chelonians". While modern looking turtles likely appeared in the Jurassic period, a few primitive turtle fossils have been discovered from Triassic period deposits.

These turtles, which lived about 220 million years ago, differed greatly from modern turtles. Not only did they lack the proper shell of modern chelonians, they had teeth embedded in their upper and lower jaws.

Because of the unique body plan of testudines (a term that refers to all the various types of turtles, including marine, terrestrial and freshwater species), scientists have long debated the group's placement within the tree of life. Those swayed by morphological data believe that turtles are most closely aligned with Lepidosaurs (a group that includes snakes, lizards and tuataras). In part, this is based on the holes (fenestra) in the skulls of ancient turtles, which resemble those present in the skulls of lizards and snakes.

However, recent genetic studies of a wide variety of species has shed light on the placement of turtles within the tree of life, as well as the placement of individual species within the turtle umbrella. (Crawford, 2012)

According to this new research, turtles are the sister group to archosaurs (a group that includes crocodilians, birds and several extinct groups, such as non-avian dinosaurs). Lepidosaurs are the sister group to the ancestor of both archosaurs and testudines (a group named the archelosauria).

This means that the closest living relatives of turtles are crocodilians and birds, rather than snakes and lizards. Nevertheless, the two groups diverged from a common path hundreds of millions of years ago. So, while the two groups are each other's closest living relatives, they are not especially closely related.

As of October 2015, scientists currently recognize 341 living testudines, but this number fluctuates as new species are discovered, different species are synonymized and subspecies are elevated to the level of full species.

Box Turtles in the Tree of Life

Herpetologists categorize all living turtles in the order Testudines. The first major division in this lineage occurs between those turtles who withdraw their neck in a lateral plane (called the sub-order Pleurodira), and those who draw their neck back in a vertical plane, called the sub-order Cryptodira.

Like most other living turtles, box turtles are members of the sub-order Cryptodira. Within this sub-order, box turtles are members of the family Emydidae, along with spotted (*Clemmys guttata*), bog (*Glyptemys muhlenbergii*), slider (*Trachemys scripta*) and painted turtles (*Chrysemys picta*).

The 10 to 12 living box turtle taxa are all members of the genus *Terrapene*. The exact classification of the various species and subspecies is debated, but one of the most common treatments recognizes the forms as:

- Eastern box turtle (*Terrapene carolina carolina*)
- Florida box turtle (*Terrapene carolina bauri*)
- Gulf Coast box turtle (*Terrapene carolina major*)
- Three-toed box turtle (*Terrapene carolina triunguis*)
- Mexican box turtle (*Terrapene carolina mexicana*)
- Yucatan box turtle (*Terrapene carolina yucatana*)
- Ornate box turtle (*Terrapene ornata ornata*)
- Desert box turtle (*Terrapene ornata luteola*)
- Nelson's box turtle (*Terrapene nelsoni*)
- Coahuila box turtle (*Terrapene coahuila*)

Chapter 4: The Environment of Box Turtles

Box turtles are generalists, who adapt to a wide variety of habitats. However, each species and subspecies lives in a different area (although some overlap commonly occurs), which is dominated by different types of habitats.

Box turtles often live in places where two or more habitats meet. These so-called "edge" habitats provide the turtles with a number of different resources. The turtles move readily between habitat types as circumstances dictate.

While box turtles are primarily terrestrial animals and do not swim exceptionally well (they have large, heavy shells and lack foot webbing), they often forage or rest in shallow water.

Basic Geography

Box turtles inhabit most of North America, from New Hampshire in the northeast, across to South Dakota and Wyoming, southwest as far as Arizona and along both coasts of Mexico, as far as the Yucatan Peninsula.

Most of the eastern varieties (*Terrapene carolina* ssp.) inhabit hardwood, pine or mixed forests, as well as wetlands, early successional areas (old fields), suburban areas, parks, riparian areas, meadows and agricultural areas.

Farther west, ornate (*Terrapene ornata ornata*) and desert box turtles (*Terrapene ornata luteola*) continue to inhabit forests and wetlands where they are present, but there is an increased use of grassy habitats, relative to their eastern counterparts.

Very little is known about the Nelson's box turtle's (*Terrapene nelsoni*) habitat preferences, but it has primarily been recorded from scrubby areas.

The Coahuila box turtle (*Terrapene coahuila*) is the most aquatic member of the genus, and they are rarely found far from water. These turtles survive in the hot, dry Mexican deserts by relying on shallow waterways to move between habitat patches. According to researchers with the University of Texas at Austin, these turtles spend about 90% of their lives in the water.

Climate
Temperatures and precipitation vary greatly over the range of box turtles. Turtles living in the northeastern United States must adapt to short activity seasons and avoid very cold winter temperatures by brumating for four to six months of the year.

However, these northeastern turtles benefit from ample rainfall. Conversely, those living in the central portions of North America must not only contend with long, cold winters; they must also find ways to survive long periods without rain.

Turtles living in the southernmost states and Mexico may be able to remain active all year long, but they must cope with sweltering summer temperatures. They can do this by burrowing under the soil and becoming relatively inactive (a behavior termed aestivation), or they can alter their diel patterns, by feeding and breeding during the morning and evening, and remaining in cool retreats during the heat of the day.

Ecology

Like all other animals, box turtles must interact with other organisms in their habitats – they do not live in a vacuum. Box turtles must live alongside countless other species, drawing resources from some and avoiding threats represented by others. Still other species play no appreciable role in the lives of these small turtles.

Vegetation

While young box turtles are primarily carnivorous, mature specimens are opportunistic omnivores, who consume a significant amount of plant material. Most of the plant matter the turtles consume comes in the form of fleshy fruits, but flowers and seeds are also potential food sources.

Although box turtles may consume lettuce, greens and other leafy food sources in captivity, a 1983 study in the Appalachian Mountains found that box turtles did not consume green leaves. (Strang, 1983) This is an interesting finding, as many other turtles and tortoises are known to consume green leaves as part of their diet.

In areas with high-temperatures and ample rainfall all year long, box turtles may feed on plant matter throughout the year. However, those living in areas with harsh winters may be limited to consuming vegetation from late spring through early fall, as the winter kills off most of the food-producing plants.

Box turtles consume a wide variety of plant species, and it is likely that their regular diet includes many foods that have yet to be recorded. However, a few of their preferred food sources include:

Blueberries (*Vaccinium* spp.)

Thatch palm fruits (*Leucothrinax* spp.)

Cherries (*Prunus* spp.)

Blackberries (*Rubus* spp.)

Mayapple fruits (*Podophyllum peltatum*)

Wild turnip fruits (*Arisaema triphyllum*)

Wild strawberries (*Fragaria vesca*)

Grapes (*Vitis* spp.)

American pokeweed fruits (*Phytolacca americana*)

Greenbrier fruits (*Smilax* spp.)

Cheese shrub fruits (*Morinda royoc*)

Figs (*Ficus* spp.)

Fan palm fruits (*Coccothrinax argentata*)

Pond apples (*Annona glabra*)

Wild guava fruits (*Mosiera longipes*)

Locust berries (*Byrsonima lucida*)

Passionflower fruits (*Passiflora* spp.)

Hackberries (*Celtis* spp.)

Sycamore seeds (*Platanus occidentalis*)

Persimmons (*Diospyros virginiana*)

Tupelo fruits (*Nyssa sylvatica*)

Saw palmetto fruits (*Serenoa repens*)

Mulberry fruits (*Morus* spp.)

Box turtles appear to be important agents of seed dispersal. Research has shown that many seeds consumed by box turtles pass through the digestive systems of the turtles and remain viable after being expelled. Some species appear to germinate more effectively after passing through a box turtle's body than they do otherwise. (Joanne Braun and Garnett R. Brooks, 1987)

Prey
Box turtles will consume virtually any small creature they can catch and overpower. The most important prey items are invertebrates, including insects, mollusks, worms and arachnids.

Earthworms, slugs and snails are likely the most important dietary items, although roaches, crickets and caterpillars are also consumed frequently.

Box turtles do consume small vertebrates from time to time, including small lizards, snakes, salamanders and frogs. They readily consume carrion, including road-killed animals. Anecdotal reports indicate that box turtles may engage in cannibalism and prey on immature turtles.

Box turtles also consume a variety of strange items, including deer feces and animal bones, which represent a bounty of calcium and other minerals.

A box turtle dines on an earthworm.

Predators

From the time they are buried in the ground as eggs, until they reach 3 to 5 years of age, box turtles have a variety of predators, representing most common lineages.

Other reptiles, such as large snakes and lizards opportunistically consume small turtles, just as predatory birds and mammals. Even animals that are normally herbivorous, such as squirrels and chipmunks, may consume small box turtles when the opportunity arises.

Once mature, box turtles are safe from all but the largest or most determined predators, such as canids, felids, raccoons and humans.

Other Associations

Wild box turtles often suffer from a variety of internal parasites, including roundworms, tapeworms and flagellate protozoans. Although these parasites rarely cause health problems for healthy box turtles, stressed, injured, malnourished or diseased specimens may succumb to such infestations.

Box turtles may also serve as hosts for a variety of fly larvae. Bot flies (*Cuterebra* spp.) will bite the skin of flies, creating an opening into which they deposit their eggs. Upon hatching, the larvae form a protective cyst, and feed on the turtle's tissues. Upon completing their development, the larvae will exit the cyst. Other flies colonize existing wounds.

Box turtles may also serve as hosts for ticks.

PART II: BOX TURTLE HUSBANDRY

Once equipped with a basic understanding of what box turtles *are* (Chapter 1 and Chapter 3), where they *live* (Chapter 4), and what they *do* (Chapter 2) you can begin learning about their captive care.

Animal husbandry is an evolving pursuit. Keepers shift their strategies frequently as they incorporate new information and ideas into their husbandry paradigms.

There are few "right" or "wrong" answers, and what works in one situation may not work in another. Accordingly, you may find that different authorities present different, and sometimes conflicting, information regarding the care of these turtles.

In all cases, you must strive to learn as much as you can about your pet and its natural habitat, so that you may provide it with the best quality of life possible.

Chapter 5: Box Turtles as Pets

Caring for any animal is a profound responsibility that requires both the means and the desire to provide it with a high quality of life. It is imperative that potential keepers understand what is involved in caring for a box turtle, in order to make a deliberate, sober decision.

Box Turtle Suitability

When provided with suitable housing, care and veterinary attention, box turtles often thrive in captive environments. The many box turtles living happy and healthy lives in zoos, museums, educational institutions and private homes around the world demonstrate this clearly.

Box turtles are small turtles, who require cages of relatively modest size. They are relatively easy to feed, adjust well to the presence of their keepers and adapt to a wide variety of husbandry protocols.

Nevertheless, box turtles do present husbandry challenges and are not suitable pets for all keepers. Box turtles require elaborate housing, including heating and lighting fixtures, substrates and hiding places.

Box turtles also live long lives, and few keepers are prepared to provide them with the proper care for multiple decades. They require daily maintenance and unusual food sources (including live insects or other feeder animals).

Box turtles suffer from a few common health problems, making it important for turtle owners to continue to learn about their pets and work closely with their veterinarian.

Captive bred animals typically harbor fewer parasites than their wild-caught counterparts do, but the majority of animals in the pet trade are wild caught. This not only means that captives may harbor parasites or disease, but it places pressure on wild populations.

Because many box turtle populations are experiencing population declines, wild caught individuals should be avoided whenever possible. While they are not for everyone, experienced keepers, with the resources, desire and dedication befitting such amazing animals, can successfully maintain these turtles in captivity.

What You'll Need

To keep a box turtle as a pet, you must provide it with all of its needs. This includes:

- A suitable enclosure
- Appropriate substrate
- Cage furniture
- Proper lighting fixtures and bulbs
- Heating equipment
- Monitoring equipment (thermometers, etc.)
- Food
- Husbandry tools (tongs, etc.)
- Transport containers
- Cage cleaning equipment and supplies

While every situation is different, a couple of fair scenarios are laid out in the following chart. These represent the initial costs of becoming a box turtle owner; they do not address on-going costs such as food and veterinary care.

Costs of Captivity

Inexpensive Option

Hatchling Box Turtle	$50 (£32)
Large Plastic Storage Box	$50 (£32)
Lid Supplies and Hardware	$20 (£13)
Heating and Lighting Equipment	$100 (£64)
Digital Indoor-Outdoor Thermometer	$15 (£9)
Infrared Thermometer	$35 (£22)
Cage Furniture	$20 (£13)
Food Dishes, Misc.	$25 (£16)
Total	$315 (£207)

Moderate Option

Adult Box Turtle	$100 (£65)
Large Pond Liner	$75 (£49)
Lid Supplies and Hardware	$25 (£16)
Heating and Lighting Equipment	$100 (£64)
Digital Indoor-Outdoor Thermometer	$15 (£9)
Infrared Thermometer	$35 (£22)
Cage Furniture	$30 (£19)
Food Dishes, Misc.	$25 (£16)
Total	$825 (£539)

Premium Option

Albino Box Turtle (price is a guess as this is a rare turtle in an unestablished market)	$5000 (£3300)
Custom Outdoor Enclosure	$250 (£165)
Digital Indoor-Outdoor Thermometer	$15 (£9)
Infrared Thermometer	$35 (£22)
Cage Furniture	$100 (£65)
Forceps, Misc.	$25 (£16)
Total	$5425 (£3577)

Myths and Misunderstandings

Before going further, it is important to distinguish between some of the myths and facts surrounding box turtles and their care.

Myth: Box turtles need friends or they will get lonely.

Fact: Box turtles primarily live solitary lives in the wild; interactions are only common among breeding adults. However, many keepers successfully house box turtles in pairs or small groups. Nevertheless, it is important to understand that even turtles that appear to coexist peacefully may be living in conflict.

Myth: Turtles grow in proportion to the size of their cage and then stop.

Fact: Reptiles do no such thing. Healthy box turtles reach 4 to 8 inches in length regardless of the size of their enclosure. Placing them in a small cage in an attempt to stunt their growth is an **unthinkably cruel practice**, which is more likely to sicken or kill your pet than stunt its growth. This is especially foolish for animals as small as box turtles – it is easy enough to provide them with an appropriate enclosure.

Myth: Box turtles can survive on any food you give them.

Fact: Diet is one of the most important components of box turtle husbandry and you must select food items very deliberately. Dietary problems often become quite serious before obvious symptoms appear and they can be very difficult – sometimes impossible – to rectify.

Myth: Reptiles have no emotions and do not suffer.

Fact: While turtles have very primitive brains, and do not have emotions comparable to those of higher mammals, they absolutely can suffer. Always treat reptiles with the same compassion you would offer a dog, cat or horse.

Myth: Box turtles are tame animals and never hurt their keepers.

Fact: While box turtles usually respond to perceived threats by hiding in their shells, frightened individuals may attempt to bite. It is also possible for box turtles to mistakenly bite the hand that feeds them, so forceps should be used to offer food.

Myth: You can tell the age of a box turtle by counting the rings on its scutes.

Fact: While you can usually get a general idea of a box turtle's age by counting the rings on its scutes, the ring number rarely matches the age of the turtle precisely. At best, a ring count provides you with an estimate of the turtle's age.

Chapter 6: Your Box Turtle's Enclosure

The first thing that you need to keep a box turtle as a pet is an enclosure – it is the defining characteristic of captivity!

Over the years, keepers have used a wide variety of enclosure types, each of which offers different benefits and drawbacks. Some keepers prefer inexpensive, functional enclosures and place a premium on things like cost, durability and ease of maintenance, while other keepers desire to build the most visually impressive habitat possible. Still others may design an enclosure well suited for captive reproduction.

Similarly, keepers differ on the space requirements of turtles; some find relatively modest cage sizes to be sufficient, while others prefer to provide their turtles with larger accommodations.

Regardless of which side of the spectrum you fall on, you must always provide your pet with an enclosure that is large enough to meet the turtle's basic needs – minimally including sufficient room to establish thermal gradients, permit exercise and allow mental stimulation for the animal.

As you proceed, consider all of the variables facing you and your pet, and design a habitat that best fits your circumstances.

Indoor or Outdoor?

The first major decision you must make with respect to the enclosure is its location. Specifically, you must decide whether you wish to keep your turtle indoors or outdoors. Both approaches have their merits and challenges, and you must decide which approach is best for your pet.

Because of their lightning needs, most turtles thrive best when kept outdoors and allowed to bask in unfiltered, natural sunlight. While reptile lighting systems have come a long way in the last few decades, no lightbulb will ever be able to produce the same quality and intensity of light as the sun does.

This is obviously not possible in all locations, but box turtles will likely thrive outdoors in any place that hosts wild box turtles. This includes the southern two-thirds of the United States (some wild populations penetrate as far north as Canada) as well as areas with similar climates, such as the warmer portions of Europe. If you live in areas with very cold temperatures, indoor maintenance is required.

However, even if the local climate is suitable for maintaining their health, outdoor housing is not without its drawbacks – particularly as it relates to immature box turtles.

Small box turtles are at greater risk to predators and less tolerant of temperature extremes than the adults are. They are also more difficult to monitor in outdoor enclosures (unless the enclosures are very small), which presents additional challenges for the keeper.

Considering all the various factors, the best path forward – and the one embraced by many box turtle keepers – is to keep your pet indoors while it is young, and then move to an outdoor husbandry regimen, once it is large enough to be safe from predators and better able to tolerate temperature extremes.

Box Turtle Safety

While mature individuals are largely safe from most predators, the list of potential suburban predators that may prey upon small box turtles includes:

- Coyotes
- Crows
- Feral cats
- Feral dogs
- Foxes
- Hawks
- Herons
- Minks
- Opossums
- Owls
- Raccoons
- Ravens
- Snakes
- Weasels

Accordingly, it is imperative that you take steps to keep small individuals safe if you choose to house your turtle outdoors.

Each of these predators relies on a different skill set to find and capture prey. This means that you may need to employ multiple safety features to protect your pet.

For example, a smooth wall 4 to 6 feet (1.2 to 1.8 meters) high surrounding the habitat will likely keep out most snakes and feral dogs, but it will do very little to keep out hawks, owls or crows. Conversely, a mesh cover with an open weave may prevent birds from dining on your turtle, but it will do little to keep out snakes.

Digging predators – dogs, weasels, foxes and others – also represent a tunneling threat; so, you must construct the wall so that it penetrates below ground level for a distance of at least 1 to 2 feet (30 to 60 centimeters).

While mature box turtles may be relatively safe from predators, determined humans may steal or harm your pet. Locks and security systems will reduce the chances of people accessing your pet, but they provide no guarantees.

Although they are not true "predators" in the strictest sense of the word, rodents may gnaw on sleeping turtles of all sizes, so you must take all reasonable measures to exclude them from the habitat.

Design and Materials

Keeping turtles indoors requires the use of a large container of some sort. Plastic storage boxes, pond liners and cattle troughs, are a few of the most commonly used items, but virtually any smooth-sided, non-toxic, durable container will work. Commercial tubs built specifically for turtles and tortoises are also available, as are more generalized commercial cages.

If you live in a pet- and child-free home, you can forgo a lid for the cage, but if small creatures have access to the habitat, a lid is necessary.

Make the lid from metal mesh or screen, which will not only provide for adequate ventilation, it will allow your lights to illuminate and heat the cage.

If you prefer, you can use commercially built, plastic reptile cages for young turtles, but they are inferior to tub-style confinement, as proper cages almost always feature transparent plastic or glass doors.

Aquariums and cages with glass doors are not appropriate for box turtles. Unfamiliar with the principle of transparent materials, the turtles often spend long periods of time trying to walk or tunnel through the invisible barrier. If allowed to continue, this behavior can lead to injuries.

For outdoor turtle maintenance, you need to build a walled-off "pen". You can make the walls out of water-sealed wood, plastic panels, cinder blocks or poured cement walls – just be sure that whatever you use has the structural stability to withstand the elements, the activity of your turtle and the wear and tear you will create as you maintain the habitat.

The walls of the enclosure must extend underground for at least 12 inches (30 centimeters), to reduce the chances of the turtles tunneling under the wall. Some keepers also find it helpful to bury wooden panels or cement around the inside perimeter of the fence, which will also help to reduce the chances of a jailbreak.

Always be sure that the interior of the enclosure is free of exposed nails, screws and other items that may harm your pet.

Layout and Size

In most cases, rectangular cage designs are superior to square or round cage designs. This is because the rectangular layout allows you to create a more effective thermal gradient in a given amount of space than a square or round layout does. Additionally, rectangular enclosures provide a longer distance that the animal can travel before reaching a barrier, which is likely to promote better health and well-being.

Nevertheless, some keepers have had great success with cages of all shapes and configurations. As long as the turtle's needs are met, any configuration will work. To some extent, you will have to customize the enclosure to suit your home or yard, given its scale.

If you are utilizing an outdoor enclosure, try to construct it in such a way that part of the enclosure receives direct sunlight, while the other portion of the enclosure lies in the shade. The grade should be relatively flat, but a slight incline is nothing to worry about, as long as your pet appears to use all areas of the cage without trouble.

Box turtle enclosures should have a large footprint, but they need not be very tall – walls that rise about 2 feet above the ground are sufficient for even the largest individuals.

The proper size for a box turtle cage or enclosure is a subject of great debate. Many authorities present conflicting suggestions. In all cases, suggested cage sizes should be considered the minimum acceptable. Larger cages are always better.

A commonly referenced guideline states that enclosures need only be five times the turtle's length long, three times the turtle's length wide, and at least two times the turtle's length in height. "Length" in these contexts refers to the length of the turtle's shell when measured in a straight line.

In other words, by this guideline, a 6-inch-long (15 centimeter) box turtle requires a 30-inch-long, 18-inch-wide, 12-inch tall (76 centimeters x 45 centimeters x 30 centimeters) enclosure. Likewise, a 2-inch-long (5 centimeter) box turtle requires a cage 10-inches-long, 6-inches-wide and 4-inches tall (25 centimeters x 15 centimeters x 10 centimeters)   .

The Zoological Association of America requires terrestrial turtles to have enclosures with an area equal to at least 10 times the area of their shell.

Therefore, if your box turtle's shell is about 2-square-inches, its habitat must provide at least 200 square inches of space (1290 square centimeters).

However, both of these recommendations still seem quite cramped for animals that may roam about a territory measured in acres (hectares) in the wild.

Accordingly, many keepers provide more room than these recommendations suggest. A 25- to 30-square-foot (2.3- to 2.8-square meter) enclosure provides roomy accommodations for a single turtle; habitats with 50-square-feet of space likely accommodate trios comfortably.

Substrate and Furniture

Now that you have decided what type of enclosure is right for you and your turtle, you can start placing the necessary items in the tank.

Substrates

Wild box turtles live on a variety of different substrates, depending on their geographic origin. In fact, most box turtles encounter different substrates during different portions of the day and year, as they travel through various microhabitats. In general, the eastern box turtle subspecies tend to live on damper, richer substrates with more leaf litter, while the western subspecies inhabit sandier habitats with less leaf litter.

Good substrates for captive box turtles are safe, easy to maintain, readily available and provide the turtle with the proper humidity level. Additionally, they should permit burrowing and digging behaviors.

Some of the best substrates for indoor box turtle maintenance include cypress mulch, fir bark, pine bark nuggets and soil. Avoid artificial turf, carpets and pure sand substrates; the former two substrates present challenges for cage hygiene, while the latter substrate is simply too dry and dusty.

Newspaper or paper towels are acceptable substrates, particularly for short-term maintenance, quarantined animals and fresh hatchlings (before moving them to their permanent home). Paper substrates do not permit burrowing activity, so it is even important to incorporate plenty of hiding spaces than usual. Paper substrates must be changed regularly, usually no less often than once per day.

Aspen shavings or chips are acceptable for short-term maintenance, but these types of substrates will rot quickly if they are allowed to get wet.

Regardless of whether you maintain your turtles indoors or outdoors, avoid using cedar-based products, which release toxic fumes that can be fatal to reptiles. While pine bark products are safe for turtle maintenance, there is some concern that pine wood shavings may release harmful or irritating fumes.

Bare dirt is likely the best substrate for box turtles housed outdoors. If kept short, grass, clover and similar vegetation is acceptable, as is a thick carpet of mulch or leaf litter. Whenever possible, offer your box turtles a variety of different substrates. For example, allow grass to grow in one-third of the enclosure, cover one-third of the enclosure in leaf litter and keep the remaining third bare.

Gravel can be a helpful substrate for damp areas, such as near the water dish, but be sure to use gravel comprised of rocks that are larger than your pet's head. This prevents him from ingesting the gravel, which can lead to health problems.

Furniture
Most reptiles feel more secure in complex habitats than they do barren boxes with no visual barriers or items to investigate. Box turtles are no exception in this regard – most wild box turtles spend much of their time in areas with abundant vegetation and cover. Place a box turtle in a cage with no furniture, and it will normally crawl head first into one of the corners.

However, you must strike a delicate balance between adding enough items to the enclosure to give your pet a sense of security and overcrowding the habitat, which makes maintenance more difficult and reduces the space available to your pet.

There are no widely accepted guidelines governing these types of decisions; you must simply experiment until you get the right proportion of furniture to open space. However, when in doubt, it is wise to err on the side of too much open space, rather than too much furniture.

Box turtles do not need climbing branches or elevated basking platforms, as many other captive reptiles do; instead, they need plenty of hiding places and visual barriers.

Things like large rocks, inverted plastic containers and hollow logs make good choices, just be sure that they are completely stable, and will not topple as your turtle tromps all over them. Additionally, monitor your pets to ensure they do not begin digging under items in such a way that could make them fall or collapse.

Plants
Live plants can be valuable components of a high-quality turtle habitat, but they are not strictly necessary. You must be sure to avoid toxic plants, as your turtle may try to eat them.

However, determining which plants are toxic to box turtles is not easy. Most of the information available has been extrapolated from data concerning dogs, cats, horses and other mammals – not chelonians. Moreover, many authorities list conflicting information.

The best approach is to utilize plants known to be safe for turtle consumption, but always consult with your veterinarian before placing any plant species in your turtle's habitat to be safe.

For example, the numerous varieties of *Brassica oleracea* (kale, broccoli, cauliflower, etc.) are safe, although they do not make good staple foods. Small mulberries (*Morus* spp.) and hibiscus plants (*Hibiscus* spp.) are also safe to grow in your pet's cage.

Most common lawn grasses are likely safe for consumption, and box turtles are relatively unlikely to consume such coarse, vegetative material. They are not grazing animals, like tortoises are; they tend to be selective about the plant material they consume, preferring things like fruits and flowers to grass and leaves.

Edible succulents, such as prickly pear cactus (*Opuntia* spp.) and aloe (*Aloe vera*), are also worthy additions to your turtle's enclosure, assuming that you live in an area where they will thrive, and are maintaining western box turtles, which are more at home in drier habitats.

Avoid using artificial plants in your turtle's cage, as they may cause health problems if ingested.

Chapter 7: Heating and Lighting the Enclosure

Ectothermic, or "cold-blooded," animals primarily heat their bodies via external sources, such as by basking in the sunlight or sitting on a warm rock.

When they cannot reach suitable temperatures, they cannot digest their food effectively, move as quickly as necessary or perform other behaviors and bodily functions.

This can lead the animal to become dormant, such as occurs during the winter; or, it can cause the animal to become ill. Therefore, to maintain any ectothermic animal, such as a box turtle, you must provide an enclosure with suitable temperatures.

Depending upon your local climate and the manner in which you house your turtle, you may need one or more heating devices as well as the necessary monitoring equipment. Additionally, you must arrange the heating equipment in such a way that you provide the captive with a range of temperatures.

Ideal Climate for Box Turtles

Box turtles have adapted to a variety of different climates across their wide range, but most individuals prefer the same basic temperature range – from the mid-70s Fahrenheit to the mid-80s Fahrenheit (24 to 30 degrees Celsius). They will remain active at temperatures slightly outside this range, but extreme temperatures will cause them to seek shelter and become inactive.

In most situations, box turtles adjust their activity levels to match the climate. However, extended periods of time at suboptimal temperatures can affect their health of cause them to become dormant.

Temperatures can and should be allowed to drop at night, just as they do in the wild. Turtles housed indoors can usually be allowed to cool to room temperature (high 60s to the low 70s Fahrenheit) overnight, as long as they are allowed to warm up properly in the daytime.

If kept within their natural range and afforded plenty of shelter and ground cover, box turtles can usually tolerate cool nighttime temperatures, as long as the days are suitably warm. However, you should either move your animals inside or ensure that they begin brumating once the nighttime temperatures fall below about 55 degrees Fahrenheit.

Thermal Gradients

One of the most basic principles of animal husbandry is to provide captives with a range of conditions, from which they can choose which is the most comfortable.

For example, it is wise to provide all captives – particularly reptiles and other ectothermic critters, who modify their temperature behaviorally – with a range of temperatures in their enclosure.

Keepers call this practice establishing a *thermal gradient*. Creating a thermal gradient is fairly simple -- you just need to place the enclosure heat source(s) at one end of the cage. This way, temperatures will gradually fall with increasing distance from the heat source.

The area closest to the heat source becomes a basking spot, while the far end of the cage serves as a cool retreat – intermediate temperatures allow your animal to fine-tune its internal temperature.

However, the temperatures of the enclosure need not be maintained in exactly this fashion; rather than a linear variation in temperatures, you can provide the turtle with several "zones" of different temperatures. This will also allow your pet to move about the enclosure and regulate his temperature. Indeed, neat, linear gradients are not always feasible when maintaining turtles outdoors. You cannot move the sun, so you are limited to shading portions of the habitat to establish a range of temperatures.

Heating Devices

You can use any of several different types of heating devices. All have different pros and cons, which make a given device work in one scenario but not another.

CAUTION: Always use care when arranging and operating heating devices and follow all of the manufacturer's instructions.

It is generally ill advised to place heating devices outdoors, where they will be exposed to the elements.

The Sun

If you plan to keep your box turtles outdoors, the sun will serve as your primary heating source. While the sun offers many benefits to both the keeper and the kept, it also provides unique challenges.

On the plus side, the sun provides the best spectrum of light possible for turtle maintenance, it is free and it requires no maintenance; but on the other hand, you have no control over this heat source.

At best, you can try to maximize the sun exposure of the enclosure by positioning it so that it catches the most hours of sunlight possible. You will still need to contend with overcast or rainy days, but, provided that these are not common, the occasional cool, dreary day will cause the turtles no harm.

Heat Lamps

Heat lamps are the most common type of heating device used by turtle keepers to provide basking spots. Given the benefits of heat lamps, this makes good sense.

When reptile keepers refer to a "heat lamp", they mean a portable light socket surrounded by a shroud. A variety of different bulbs can be screwed into the receptacle. For example, some keepers prefer to use regular, incandescent light bulbs, while others prefer mercury vapor bulbs.

It is easy to adjust the temperature underneath a heat lamp by either changing the distance between the light and the substrate or swapping out the bulb for a different wattage.

Ceramic Heat Emitters

Ceramic heat emitters are used in place of a light bulb in a heat lamp fixture. However, unlike a light bulb, ceramic heat emitters produce no light. They only produce heat, which emanates from the ceramic.

On the plus side, most manufacturers claim that ceramic heat emitters are much more efficient than light bulbs. Additionally, as they produce no light, they can be used to heat the enclosure at night, without disturbing your pet's circadian rhythms.

However, ceramic heat emitters also have negative characteristics. Because they produce no light, you cannot tell if it is on or not by looking at it. This can lead to injuries if you accidentally touch it while it is on.

Ceramic heat emitters are also rather expensive, although when the efficiency and lifespan of the device is taken into consideration, this difference may become insignificant.

Heat Tape
Heat tape is plastic-covered electrical wire that is designed to heat up when current is applied. Heat tape is not appropriate for creating a basking spot, but it may help to keep indoor enclosures at the desired level, when placed underneath the habitat. However, you must be sure to allow air to flow across the heat tape to prevent a dangerous buildup of heat.

Heat tape is largely inappropriate for beginning reptile keepers, as it must be wired by hand. You must use heat tape with a thermostat or rheostat to maintain the proper temperatures. If you do not, the heat tape will become much too hot and may cause a fire.

Care must be used when laying out heat tape, as improper placement can represent a fire hazard – always follow the manufacturer's instructions when assembling or using heat tape.

Heat Pads
Heating pads made for reptiles are generally constructed by enclosing a length of pre-wired heat tape in a plastic cover. Like heat tape, heat pads are not helpful for maintaining a basking spot, but they may help heat the substrate if placed below the cage. Be sure that the manufacturer's instructions

permit this type of use before using a heat pad in this manner.

Heating pads should always be used with a thermostat or rheostat to maintain appropriate temperatures.

Heat Cables

Heat cables are long conducting wires that heat up when current is applied to them. Most heat cables are covered in plastic, which may or may not make them suitable for use outdoors or in situations in which they become damp.

Like heat tape or heating pads, you must use heat cables with a rheostat or, preferably, a thermostat.

Radiant Heat Panels

Radiant heat panels are similar to heating pads, except that they are designed to project heat rather than warm things that are in contact with the device. Additionally, radiant heat panels are usually placed on the ceiling or wall of an enclosure. This makes them very helpful for providing a basking spot.

Radiant heat panels often cost more than heat lamps do, but they provide safer, more controlled heat. However, radiant heat panels must be used with a thermostat to ensure they do not overheat.

Heated Rocks and Other Items

Heated rocks, branches, caves and other items were some of the earliest and most popular commercial heating devices for pet reptiles. They are made from a faux rock (or stick, etc.) and an internal heating element.

In previous decades, heated rocks garnered a bad reputation for burning reptiles. In some cases, this was due to faulty equipment, but in many others, it was due to keeper error.

These types of devices are not designed to raise the temperature of a pet reptile's habitat – they are merely designed to provide a localized basking spot. Unfortunately, many early keepers did not understand this, and so their pet reptiles wrapped tightly around these devices, while sitting in a woefully under heated cage.

Newer designs feature built-in rheostats or thermostats and are often constructed with better components. Nevertheless, they are inappropriate for turtles of any kind, and should be avoided.

Monitoring and Control Equipment

Maintaining an appropriate climate in your pet's enclosure often requires some trial and error, but this does not mean that you should blindly approach the task.

Instead, you must measure the cage temperatures, to ensure they are within the comfortable range for your pet.

Thermometers

Turtle keepers need two different types of thermometers to monitor their pet's environment properly: one to measure the ambient air temperatures and another to measure the surface temperatures of objects in the habitat.

Several different types of thermometers are appropriate for measuring the ambient air temperature, including analog and digital varieties. Often, digital, indoor-outdoor models are the best choice, as they feature a remote sensing probe. These probes allow you to monitor the temperature in two different portions of the habitat simultaneously, such as the basking spot and the burrow.

To measure the surface temperatures in the enclosure – such as the basking spot or the top of your pet's shell while he is under the basking spot – use an infrared, non-contact thermometer. Dedicated keepers often find these tools immensely valuable; invest in a quality unit, as you are likely to end up using it quite often.

Avoid the plastic, "stick-on" variety of thermometer often sold in pet stores.

Rheostats
Rheostats are akin to "volume controls" for heating devices. They work like lamp dimmer switches, as they reduce the amount of electricity reaching the heating device. This reduction in electricity reduces the amount of heat produced by the device.

Rheostats are helpful tools as they allow you to fine-tune the amount of heat supplied by a given device. However, you must still monitor the temperatures regularly, to ensure the cage temperatures stay within the desired range.

Thermostats
Thermostats are similar to rheostats, but they automatically adjust the amount of electricity reaching the heating device, in order to maintain a pre-selected temperature. Several different types of thermostats are available commercially.

Some work by simply switching the power to the heating device on and off. Others work by continually adjusting the amount of electricity reaching the device.

The former are called on-off thermostats while the later are termed pulse-proportional thermostats. On-off thermostats are only suitable for use with heat pads, radiant heat panels or heat tape.

While you must regularly check to ensure your thermostats are working, they are very helpful for maintaining proper cage temperatures, and they largely automate climate control.

Some thermostats feature a night-drop function, which allows you to program the unit to drop the temperatures by a preselected amount each night.

Thermostat Failure
Eventually, all thermostats will fail. Whether this occurs a week after you purchase the unit or 30 years from now remains to be seen, but you must prepare for the possibility.

In a worst-case scenario, thermostat failure can lead to the death of your animals.

You can provide yourself with some protection from thermostat failure by purchasing a high-quality unit, crafted from quality components. However, even expensive thermostats can fail.

Another option is to use two thermostats, wired in series. To accomplish this, you must set the primary thermostat to the preferred temperature range for your animal. You then attach a second thermostat behind the first. Set this thermostat to a few degrees higher than the primary thermostat.

This way, when the primary thermostat fails, the secondary thermostat will allow the temperature to rise a few degrees, but will prevent the habitat from becoming dangerously warm.

Nighttime Heating
If the nighttime temperatures in your area (or your home) do not fall lower than the mid-60s, you can probably avoid providing any form of heat during the nights.

It is also important to remember that the temperatures in your pet's burrow or shelters will be more moderate (warmer in cool weather, cooler in hot weather) than the ambient, aboveground temperatures.

Nevertheless, turtles should be provided with a significant temperature drop each night, as constantly warm conditions are unnatural and potentially harmful. Among other benefits provided by diel temperature swings is that they can inhibit bacterial and fungal growth. It also allows the turtles metabolic rate slow down for a period each day, which likely provides health benefits.

Differing Thermal Requirements
Like most other types of animals, small turtles are less tolerant of temperature extremes than large turtles are. In addition, because they have greater surface-to-volume ratios than larger turtles do, small individuals change temperatures much more quickly than their larger counterparts do.

Accordingly, it is wise to keep the maximum temperatures available to small turtles a few degrees below that provided to large individuals, and to keep the minimum temperatures a few degrees higher than those that are provided to large turtles.

Lighting

Most turtles require very specific lighting to remain healthy. Without it, pet turtles may develop shell irregularities, lose bone mass or suffer kidney failure, among other problems.

The easiest way to solve this problem is by maintaining your turtle outdoors. But this is not always possible, and is not ideal for young animals, who are vulnerable to predators. Therefore, in lieu of natural sunlight, keepers should provide pet turtles with high quality, "full-spectrum" lighting. Full spectrum lighting refers to lights that produce not only visible light, but light in the UV portion of the range.

More specifically, turtles generally require lights that produce light in both the UVA and UVB portions of the range. UVA is defined as light between 320 and 400 nanometers, while UVB is defined as light between 290 and 320 nanometers.

UVC, which has wavelengths of between 100 and 290 nanometers, is destructive to cells, and is not produced by bulbs designed for reptile cages or general illumination.

UVA wavelengths have been shown to influence the vision and behavior of reptiles, and may play a role in food recognition. UVB wavelengths have widely been shown to allow reptiles to convert inactive vitamin D to the active form (Vitamin D3).

Vitamin D3 is crucial to the metabolism of calcium. When reptiles are deficient in vitamin D3, they tend to draw calcium from their bones. This leads to soft bones, and is termed metabolic bone disease. Often, the condition proves fatal, or becomes debilitating enough to require euthanasia.

Once the symptoms of metabolic bone disease present themselves, the disease is often in an advanced state.

Most full spectrum lights are fluorescent bulbs. Both conventional and compact styles are available. Minimally, you must incorporate full spectrum bulbs over the basking site, but you can place them along the entire length of the enclosure if you prefer. However, if you choose to illuminate the entire tank with full-spectrum bulbs, be sure to offer the turtle refuges, where it can avoid the light.

The amount of UVB light emanating from the bulb dissipates rapidly with increasing distance from the lamp. This means that you must place the lights relatively close to the basking reptile – a maximum of about 12 inches (30 centimeters).

Full spectrum lights lose their ability to produce UVB over time, so you must replace them regularly. Follow the manufacturer's instruction regarding replacement schedule, but most lights last between 6 and 12 months.

Plug the full-spectrum lights into a lamp timer to keep your pet's photoperiod consistent. Box turtles inhabit a range of latitudes; those living at the northern extent of their range experience rather dramatic annual variation in daylight, while those living in Central America or southern Florida experience relatively little annual variation.

It is probably most helpful (and easiest on your pet) to recreate the seasonal variation characteristic of the turtle's home range in captivity. However, some keepers have success by keeping their pets under a daylight variation pattern characteristic of the keeper's location.

Of course, if you maintain your turtles outdoors, you will have no control of the photoperiod.

An attractively marked ornate box turtle.

Chapter 8: Water and Humidity

Like all animals, box turtles require liquid water to survive. Proper hydration is critical for the health of these animals, so it is important to provide fresh drinking water for your pet. Additionally, some keepers provide their turtles with periodic baths or water dishes that permit soaking, to further ensure they remain hydrated.

Drinking Water

The easiest way to provide box turtles with water is via a large, flat, shallow dish. Avoid deep, narrow water containers, as they are difficult for the turtles to access and more likely to spill. Additionally, because box turtles are not especially strong swimmers, it is imperative to avoid offering water in a dish deep enough to cause them to drown.

Plastic plant saucers, cat litter pans and plastic storage boxes make effective water dishes for adults, while small glass saucers, storage box lids or commercial water dishes designed for small turtles work best for young individuals.

Always keep the water clean to prevent your turtle from becoming sick. Wash the water dish every day with soap and water, but be sure to rinse it thoroughly before returning it to the enclosure. It is also wise to disinfect the water dish periodically by soaking it in a mild bleach solution for 1 hour and then rinsing it well.

Many keepers use tap water for their turtles, but others prefer to use bottled spring water instead. It is possible that some of the chemicals found in tap water are harmful for your pet, so consult with your veterinarian before using tap water for your pet's drinking needs.

Wading Pool

Many box turtles live in habit areas near a permanent water source; some even forage in the water regularly. Accordingly, some keepers provide their box turtle with a water vessel large enough to accommodate the turtle's entire body.

While spacious water receptacles are not strictly necessary, they provide further mental stimulation for your pet and help keep it hydrated. However, doing so increases the amount of labor necessary for routine maintenance, as you must keep the water exceptionally clean.

Do not offer box turtles a water feature that is more than 1 to 2 inches deep, to help guard against drowning – box turtles are rarely skilled swimmers.

Soaking

In addition to providing water for drinking or wading, many turtle keepers soak their pets periodically in a small bit of water. This helps to ensure they remain hydrated and often helps to dislodge dirt, grime or food stuck to the bottom of their shell.

Soak your box turtle by adding a small amount of water to a plastic storage container, bucket or similar enclosure. Only add enough water to wet the bottom of the turtle's shell – never make your pet swim or struggle to keep his head above the water. This equates to about ¼ to ½ inch for hatchlings, and about 1 inch for large adults.

Avoid using water that is substantially warmer or cooler than your pet's body temperature. One easy way to accomplish this is by placing the soaking container (with lukewarm water already added) into your pet's enclosure for about an hour before soaking him. This way, the water will be roughly the same temperature as the ambient temperatures in the cage, which will prevent your pet from becoming chilled or burned.

A typical soaking regimen may call for you to soak your turtle for 20 minutes, twice per week, although some keepers provide soaks more or less frequently than this. In all cases, it is important to monitor your turtle while he is soaking to avoid accidents.

Note that your turtle may defecate in the water. If this happens, you must change the water immediately to prevent your pet from drinking the contaminated water.

Dry your turtle off with paper towels after soaking him, which will help keep the substrate from sticking to his shell.

Humidity

Though some box turtles hail from dry regions, they spend a lot of time in their burrows and in mesic microhabitats, where the relative humidity is much higher than elsewhere.

Eastern box turtle subspecies will benefit from a moderately humid enclosure, while western subspecies may fall ill if kept in excessively humid habitats.

The easiest way to increase the humidity in the habitat is by misting the substrate and cage walls with lukewarm water. You will have to adjust the frequency of these mistings as well as the amount of water discharged at a time, to keep the habitat suitable.

You can also simply pour water into the substrate, and let the water evaporate into the air, but care must be taken to avoid allowing portions of the substrate to become soggy.

Rather than using a hygrometer, you should learn how to monitor the cage humidity by noting the feel and odor of the air. After misting, the habitat should resemble a forest after a shower.

However, you want the habitat to dry out over the next few hours. Standing water (excluding the water dish) should evaporate before the heat sources are turned off for the night.

However, they will not thrive in enclosures that are kept continually humid. This may lead to skin lesions and respiratory infections. Accordingly, it is important to provide your turtle with access to both low- and high-humidity areas within their enclosure.

One of the wisest approaches is to provide your turtle with a well-ventilated habitat, and a "damp retreat," which your pet will use as a hiding place.

You can make a damp retreat by simply placing an inverted plastic container (with a door cut into the side to provide access for the turtle) inside the cage and dampening the substrate below it.

Chapter 9: Diet

Diet is one of the most important aspects of box turtle maintenance. Many new keepers are shocked to learn that these animals require more that lettuce scraps and the odd earthworm to stay healthy. Good health requires a diet that mimics their natural diet.

Box turtles are generalist omnivores, who exploit a variety of food sources in the wild. Although the diet of different subspecies varies slightly, most will thrive on a relatively similar collection of items.

Most box turtles subsist primarily on live animal prey, but they also consume carrion, fungi and plant material.

Try to provide your pet with the broadest selection of acceptable foods possible. Most box turtles (particularly hatchlings and western subspecies) consume more animal-based food than plant- or fungus-based foods.

Food Selection

Try to provide your box turtle with as much dietary variety as is possible to help avoid nutritional deficiencies, and to provide greater mental stimulation.

Live Invertebrates
Crickets
Mealworms
Superworms
Wax Worms
Silkworms
Roaches
Grasshoppers

Slugs
Snails
Earthworms

Other Animal-Based Foods
Prekilled Rodents
Live Minnows
Fresh Fish
Cooked eggs

Fruits and Vegetables
Strawberries
Blueberries
Blackberries
Raspberries
Banana
Apples
Pears
Bell peppers
Peas
Green beans

Fungi
A variety of different fungi make up an important part of the diets of some box turtles. In fact, many box turtles consume species that would kill a human. However, you should always err on the side of caution, and only provide your turtles with commercially produced, edible varieties, such as you would find at a grocery store.

Commercial Foods

A variety of commercially produced foods are available for box turtles. The nutritional quality of these foods varies from one manufacturer to the next, so be sure to scrutinize the nutritional information provided closely.

While it is probably safe to provide these foods to your pet box turtle, they should only represent a small portion of the overall diet.

Feeding Frequency and Quantity

In addition to feeding your turtle a diverse selection of healthy foods, you must feed your pet the correct amount of food to ensure good health.

Unlike some other species (particularly tortoises of grasslands), who subsist on low-calorie grasses and other plants, box turtles consume many high-calorie foods. This means that mature box turtles can become overweight if provided with too much food (young box turtles are unlikely to become overweight, as long as they are provided with appropriate temperatures and sufficient room for exercise).

Box turtles likely feed every day or every other day in the wild, and a similar feeding strategy makes sense for captives. Offer your pets as much food as they can eat in about 5 to 10 minutes and then remove the uneaten portion.

The exact caloric needs of your pet will vary based on its gender, age, size, activity level and the foods you offer. Accordingly, you must monitor your pet to provide the ideal amount of food.

Track your turtle's growth to help ensure he receives enough food. Young animals should grow at a slow, yet consistent rate, while adults may eventually cease growing, they should maintain their body weight.

Preparing Food for Your Turtle

While a little dirt is unlikely to sicken your turtle, it makes sense to keep their food as clean as possible. Bacteria, fungi and parasites likely litter the ground of your pet's enclosure, so use a clean food dish or flat rock for your pet's meals.

While it is not strictly necessary to do so, most keepers cut or shred foods for small turtles to make it easier for them to eat. However, this is more important for some foods than it is for others. For example, even the smallest hatchlings can handle hibiscus flowers, but strawberries and other large fruits are difficult for small turtles to handle.

Vitamin and Mineral Supplementation

Many keepers supplement their box turtle's diet with vitamin and mineral powders. Presumably, this type of dietary supplementation helps to offset deficiencies caused by an improper diet.

However, as these products are not without risk, it is preferable to avoid this necessity, by providing your pet with a nutritionally balanced diet that mimics their natural diet.

The problems inherent to supplements include the difficulties involved in providing a correct dosage, uncertainty over the correct levels of supplementation necessary and potential problems with palatability – some turtles may not consume foods that have been supplemented.

Many vitamins and minerals are toxic in excessive quantities, and, veterinarians have yet to establish clear dosages and guidelines. In fact, these dietary needs surely vary with age; for example, young turtles and egg-laying females undoubtedly require more calcium in their diet than mature males do. Failing to take these considerations into account can lead to health problems for your turtle.

In light of these facts, it becomes apparent that the best strategy for box turtle maintenance is to provide a diet that mimics their natural diet as closely as is possible and includes plenty of variety, which will likely reduce the chances of vitamin or mineral deficiencies. Then, discuss the potential need for supplementation with your veterinarian and follow his or her advice.

Chapter 10: Monitoring and Maintenance

Once you have set up your turtle's home, you must work to keep it habitable for your pet. Most illnesses in captive reptiles spring from inappropriate husbandry (particularly the failure to keep the habitat suitably clean), so be vigilant about maintaining the habitat to avoid such problems.

Cleaning Techniques and Supplies
Some of the things you may need to maintain the habitat include:

- Paper towels
- Soap-free scrub pads
- Heavy-duty, plastic bristled scrub brush
- Wire scrub brush
- Bleach
- Measuring cups
- Spray bottles
- Long-handled scrubbing tool

Maintenance Schedule
Try to establish a regular maintenance routine. Some tasks are necessary on a daily basis, while other tasks can be performed less frequently.

Daily

- Visually inspect the habitat and turtle, looking for any problems with the habitat or health concerns.
- Be sure that the habitat remains secure and that your pet cannot escape.

- Ensure that the temperatures in the habitat are within the appropriate range.
- Clean the habitat, removing any feces, urates, uneaten food or other such items from the enclosure.
- Empty, clean and refill the water dish.

Weekly

- Inspect outdoor habitats to be sure that no noxious or toxic plants have sprouted in or near the enclosure.
- Check for signs of pests, such as rodents, ants or roaches.
- Inspect any burrows or hiding spots in the cage to ensure they remain clean and safe.

Monthly

- Break down indoor habitats completely, replacing the substrate and cleaning all interior cage surfaces.
- Replace plants or cage furniture as necessary.
- Weigh and measure your turtle. This is particularly important with young turtles, so that you can monitor their growth. If your turtle is mature, and healthy, you can weigh and measure it less frequently.

Annually

- Change full-spectrum bulbs in indoor cages (some bulbs require replacement every 6 months – consult the manufacturer's instructions).
- Inspect all of the electrical cords, light fixtures and all other equipment for signs of wear.

Records

Proper record keeping is a crucial, but often neglected, aspect of reptile husbandry. Unfortunately, too many keepers neglect this simple and important practice.

Written records allow you to note trends, anticipate problems before they occur and learn from prior mistakes. By reviewing your husbandry records with your veterinarian, you may be able to figure out why a given health problem is occurring.

You can keep records in virtually any way you like. Some prefer to use elaborate record-keeping software packages, while others prefer to take handwritten notes, as with a journal. Either of these options – or any other option that suits your needs – is acceptable. The important thing is that you keep records.

You can never record too much data, but always record the source of your new pet, the date on which you acquired the turtle, and its weight (and length if possible) at the time of acquisition.

ID Number :	44522	Genus: Species /Sub:	Terrap ene ornata	Gender : DOB:	? 3/20 /15	CA RD #2
6.30.1 5 Cricke ts	7.03.1 5 Cricke ts, Superw orms	7.08.15 Apple slices	7.14.1 5 Strawb erry	7.17.1 5 Cricke ts		
7.01.1 5 Cricke ts	7.05.1 5 Earthw orms	7.09.15 Roaches	7.15.1 5 Superw orms, Roache s	7.19.1 5 Earthw orms		

7.02.15 Blueberries	7.06.15 Crickets	7.12.15 Earthworms	7.16.15 Crickets			

Date	Notes
6-22-13	Acquired ""Box-Car-Joe" the ornate box turtle from a turtle breeder named Mark at the in-town reptile expo. Mark explained that Joe's scientific name is Terrapene ornata. Cost was $50. Mark was not sure what sex Joe was, and wasn't sure how to tell. Mark said he hatched the turtle in March, but he does not know the exact date.
6-23-13	I have decided to consider Joe a boy until he gets big enough to know for sure. He spent the night in the container I bought him in. I purchased a 20-gallon plastic tub and a thermometer at the hardware store and a bag of substrate and a heat lamp at the pet store. Bought a non-contact thermometer online. I am using old food containers for his water dish. I added an upside down tub with a door cut into it for a hide.
6-27-13	Joe hid in his shell when I misted him. He ate a ton of crickets! At least 10.
6-30-13	I fed Joe a thawed hopper mouse today. I have never seen anything so gross in my life! He got mouse guts all over the cage, so I had to put him in his holding tub and clean the entire cage.
7-2-13	Two blueberries today. He didn't seem very hungry – probably still digesting that mouse.
7-5-13	Fed Joe a dozen crickets and a moth that flew into the house. I killed the moth before giving it to him, but he didn't seem to mind. He ate everything and looked like he wanted more.

Chapter 11: Acquiring a Box Turtle

Now that you have decided to get a box turtle, and you understand the care it requires, it is time to find your pet. Modern reptile enthusiasts can acquire box turtles from a variety of sources, each with a different set of pros and cons.

PRO TIP: It is easy to get over excited about the potential of a new pet, which can lead to hasty decisions and regret. Take your time and select the perfect turtle for you. You will have your pet for the next several decades; you can take a few weeks to find the ideal companion.

Pet Stores

Pet stores are a common source for many beginning turtle keepers, but they are not always the best place to purchase your new pet.

The benefits of shopping at a pet store are that they usually have all of the equipment to care for your new turtle, including cages, heating devices and food items. You will usually be able to inspect the animal up close before purchase. In some cases, you may be able to choose from more than one specimen.

Many pet stores provide health guarantees for a short period, which provides you with some recourse if your new pet turns out to be ill. However, pet stores are retail establishments, and as such, you will pay more than you will from a breeder.

The drawbacks to purchasing a turtle from a pet store relate to the amount of expertise and knowledge of the staff. While some pet stores concentrate on reptiles and may have a staff capable of providing them with proper care, many turtles languish while living in pet stores. Pet stores do not often know the pedigree of the animals they sell, nor are they likely to know the turtle's date of birth, or other pertinent information.

It is also worth considering the increased exposure to pathogens that pet store animals endure, given the constant flow of animals through the facility.

Reptile Expos

Reptile expos *can be* excellent places to acquire new animals. Reptile expos often feature resellers, breeders and retailers in the same room, all selling various types of turtles and other reptiles.

Often, the prices at such events are quite reasonable and you are often able to select from many different turtles. However, reptile expos are not without their problems.

For example, if you have a problem with your new pet, it may be difficult to find the seller after the event is over. Do not assume that a given vendor is skilled and reputable just because they have paid for a table at the event. Use your critical thinking skills and research the vendor as much as possible (you can likely do an internet search from your phone while you are speaking with him or her), before making the purchase.

Breeders

Breeders are the best place for most novices to shop for turtles. Breeders generally offer unparalleled information and support after the sale. Additionally, breeders often know the species well, and are better able to help you learn the husbandry techniques for the animal.

The disadvantage of buying from a breeder is that you must often make such purchases from a distance, either by phone or via the internet. Breeders often have the widest selection of turtles, and are often the only place to find rare forms and truly spectacular specimens.

Classified Advertisements

Newspaper and website classified advertisements sometimes include listings for turtles. While individuals, rather than businesses generally post these, they are viable options to monitor. Often, these sales include the turtle and all of the associated equipment, which is convenient for new keepers. However, be careful to avoid purchasing someone else's "problem" (i.e. a sick or maladapted turtle).

Selecting Your Turtle

Not all turtles are created equally – you want to be careful in selecting the best specimen you can find. While you can consider color or other aesthetic qualities in your selection process, they should be minor concerns. Only select turtles that appear healthy.

Health Checklist
Never purchase a box turtle displaying any of the following signs or symptoms:

- Lumps, swellings or ulcers

- Puffy or closed eyes
- Shell deformations or wounds
- Limb or tail deformations
- Overgrown beak
- Discharge from the eyes
- Discharge from the nostrils or mouth
- Discharge from the vent

If possible, observe the turtle walking on the ground. Healthy box turtles should move easily, and be alert and active. If the turtle is small enough to be held, it should feel heavy for its size; sick turtles often feel very light.

The Gender

Whenever possible, select male box turtles for pets. While it is true that males grow to larger sizes than females do, which is not always ideal, males do not present any of the reproductive-related challenges females do.

Female turtles – even those who are not housed with males – may produce eggs. If they cannot find a suitable egg deposition site, they may become egg bound. This can necessitate expensive and invasive surgeries, or lead to death.

Captive Bred Vs. Wild Caught

For a litany of reasons, captive bred box turtles are unquestionably superior pets to wild caught specimens.

Whereas captive bred individuals are usually healthy and well-adapted to the captive environment, wild caught individuals are often heavily parasitized, stressed, malnourished and dehydrated. Many bear the scars typical of a life spent dealing with the threats of the wild.

While it is possible for experienced keepers to overcome these challenges and nurse these individuals back to health, novices will usually struggle.

Another problem with wild caught turtles is that these animals have been removed from the wild. This places wild populations – and in some cases, entire taxa -- at risk of extinction.

Unfortunately, most box turtles available in the market are wild caught adults, but captive bred animals can be found with some effort on the part of the keeper.

An exceptionally orange eastern box turtle.

Chapter 12: Interacting with Your Box Turtle

You must be sure that your interactions with your turtle are safe and positive for all parties involved. Contact with a large predator (such as yourself) may cause the turtle stress, which can lead to illness and maladaptation. Additionally, improper handling can cause your pet to suffer injuries.

In general, this means that you should avoid most unnecessary physical contact with your pet. However, you need to observe your turtle for signs of illness regularly, and this will occasionally necessitate directly handling or manipulating the animal.

Handling Your Turtle

The best way to hold hatchling box turtles is by placing your index finger on top of the animal's carapace and placing your thumb under its plastron. Do not pinch the shell too firmly, as young turtle shells lack the rigidity of adult shells.

When holding larger individuals, use the thumb one side of the shell and three or four fingers on the opposite. For truly large individuals, you may want to employ the use of both hands.

Never use a turtle's tail to support its bodyweight, as it can lead to spinal injuries.

Transporting Your Turtle

From time to time, it will be necessary to transport your pet. When doing so, you must keep the turtle protected from injury, within the appropriate temperature range and protected from sources of stress.

The best way to do so is by placing your turtle in a plastic storage box, filled with a soft layer of newspaper or mulch. Opaque boxes will keep your turtle calmer, while transparent boxes will allow you to observe the animal without opening the lid.

Be sure to drill a few ventilation holes on each of the container's vertical sides so that your pet can breathe easily. When drilling the holes, drill from the inside of the tub toward the outside, to prevent any sharp edges from contacting your turtle.

Hygiene

Turtles often carry various strains of *Salmonella* bacteria, as well as other harmful pathogens. While these bacteria rarely cause illness in the turtles, they can make humans – particularly those with compromised immune systems – very ill. In tragic cases, death can result from such infections.

Accordingly, it is imperative to employ sound hygiene practices when caring for a pet turtle. In general, this means:

- Always wash your hands with soap and warm water following any contact with your pet, the enclosure or items that have contacted either.
- Never wash turtle cages, furniture or tools in sinks or bathtubs used by humans.
- Never perform any husbandry tasks in kitchens or bathrooms used by humans.

- Keep high-risk individuals, such as those who are less than 5 years of age, elderly, pregnant or otherwise immunocompromised, away from captive turtles and their habitats.

Chapter 13: Box Turtle Health

Like many other turtles, box turtles are remarkably hardy animals, who often remain healthy despite their keeper's mistakes. In fact, most illnesses that befall pet turtles result from improper husbandry, and are therefore, entirely avoidable.

Nevertheless, like most other reptiles, box turtles often fail to exhibit any symptoms that they are sick until they have reached an advanced state of illness. This means that prompt action is necessary at the first hint of a problem. Doing so provides your pet with the greatest chance of recovery.

While proper husbandry is solely in the domain of the keeper, and some minor injuries or illnesses can be treated at home, veterinary care is necessary for many health problems.

Finding a Suitable Vet

While any veterinarian – even one who specializes in dogs and cats – may be able to help you keep your pet happy, it is wise to find a veterinarian who specializes in treating reptiles. Such veterinarians are more likely to be familiar with your pet species and be familiar with the most current treatment standards for reptiles.

Some of the best places to begin your search for a reptile-oriented veterinarian include:

- Veterinary associations
- Local pet stores
- Local colleges and universities

It is always wise to develop a relationship with a qualified veterinarian before you need his or her services. This way, you will already know where to go in the event of an emergency, and your veterinarian will have developed some familiarity with your pet.

When to See the Vet

Most conscientious keepers will not hesitate to seek veterinary attention on behalf of their pet. However, veterinary care can be expensive for the keeper and stressful for the kept, so unnecessary visits are best avoided.

If you are in doubt, call your veterinarian and explain the problem. He or she can then advise you if the problem requires an office visit or not.

However, you must always seek prompt veterinary care if your pet exhibits any of the following signs or symptoms:

- Traumatic injuries, such as lacerations, burns, broken bones, cracked shells or puncture wounds
- Sores, ulcers, lumps or other deformations of the skin
- Intestinal disturbances that do not resolve within 48 hours
- Drastic change in behavior
- Inability to deposit eggs

Remember that reptiles are perfectly capable of feeling pain and suffering, so apply the golden rule: If you would appreciate medical care for an injury or illness, it is likely that your pet does as well.

Common Health Problems

The following are some of the most common health problems that afflict turtles – especially box turtles. Be alert for any signs of the following maladies, and take steps to remedy the problem.

Respiratory Infections

Respiratory infections are some of the most common illnesses that afflict turtles and other captive reptiles.

The most common symptoms of respiratory infections are discharges from the nose or mouth; however, lethargy, inappetence and behavioral changes (such as basking more often than normal) may also accompany respiratory infections.

Myriad causes can lead to this type of illness, including communicable pathogens, as well as, ubiquitous, yet normally harmless, pathogens, which opportunistically infect stressed animals.

Your turtle may be able to fight off these infections without veterinary assistance, but it is wise to solicit your vet's opinion at the first sign of illness. Some respiratory infections can prove fatal and require immediate attention.

Your vet will likely obtain samples, send of the samples for laboratory testing and then interpret the results. Antibiotics or other medications may be prescribed to help your turtle recover, and your veterinarian will likely encourage you to keep the turtle's stress level low, and ensure his enclosure temperatures are ideal.

In fact, it is usually a good idea to raise the temperature of the basking spot upon first suspecting that your turtle is suffering from a respiratory infection. Elevated body temperatures (such as those that occur when mammals have fevers) help the turtle's body to fight the infection, and many will bask for longer than normal when ill.

Metabolic Bone Disease

Metabolic bone disease (MBD) is a complicated phenomenon that befalls turtles who are provided with insufficient calcium or insufficient amounts of the active form of vitamin D (D3), which is necessary for calcium utilization.

A well-rounded, diverse diet with plenty of grasses and weeds helps to ensure your pet receives enough calcium. Additionally, many keepers supplement their turtle's food items with calcium powders. However, it is important to consult with your veterinarian to devise a suitable supplementation schedule, as providing too much calcium can be just as problematic as providing too little.

A balanced diet will provide your turtle with plenty of inactive vitamin D. To allow your pet to convert this into the active form, you must provide it with exposure to ultraviolet radiation (specifically UVB). This can be accomplished either by housing your turtle outdoors and allowing them to bask in natural sunlight, or by illuminating their enclosure with full spectrum lights that produce light in the UVB portion of the spectrum.

When deprived of proper lighting, the calcium levels in the turtle's blood fall. This causes the turtle's body to draw calcium from the bones (including the shell) to rectify the problem.

As calcium is removed from the bones, they become soft and flexible, rather than hard and rigid. This can lead to broken bones or disfigurement, which can leave your turtle unable to eat, walk or swim.

Advanced cases of MBD are rarely treatable, and euthanasia is often the only humane option. However, when caught early and treated aggressively, some of the symptoms of the disease can be stopped. Accordingly, it is of the upmost importance to seek veterinary care at the first sign of MBD.

Shell Rot
Shell rot is a catchall term for a variety of maladies related to a turtle's shell. Shell rot normally takes the form of lesions or ulcers; sometimes, a small amount of fluid may leak from the wounds.

Shell rot may occur because of a systematic infection or as a local phenomenon. Bacteria or fungi may be the primary cause of the problem, or injuries may provide an opportunity for pathogens to colonize the tissues.

Shell rot is usually treatable with prompt veterinary care, so always see your veterinarian at the first sign of problems.

Parasites
Parasites are rare among captive-bred box turtles, but poor husbandry can cause them to become a problem. Parasites rarely become problematic for wild turtles, unless they become injured, stressed or ill.

Most internal parasites cause intestinal problems, such as runny or watery stools, vomiting or decreased appetites. Your veterinarian can collect blood or stool samples from your turtle, analyze them to determine what parasites, if any, are present, and prescribe medications to clear the infestation. Often, multiple treatments are necessary to eradicate the parasites completely.

External parasites afflict box turtles on occasion, usually in the form of ticks. Because some ticks carry dangerous diseases, you should have your veterinarian inspect any animal carrying the parasitic arthropods.

Anorexia

Box turtles are normally ravenous eaters, who rarely pass up the chance to consume calories. However, they may refuse food if ill, if kept in suboptimal temperatures (including seasonally cool temperatures, such as occur during the winter) or are preoccupied by breeding.

Refusing a meal or two is not cause for alarm, but if your turtle refuses food for longer than this, be sure to review your husbandry practices. If the turtle continues to refuse food without an obvious reason for doing so, consult your veterinarian.

Injuries

Despite their protective shells box turtles can become injured in myriad ways, including battles with cagemates, overly zealous breeding attempts, or by sustaining burns from heaters. While turtles are likely to heal from most minor wounds without medical attention, serious wounds will necessitate veterinary assistance.

Your vet will likely clean the wound, make any repairs necessary (shell patches, sutures, etc.) and prescribe a course of antibiotics to help prevent infection. Be sure to keep the enclosure as clean as possible during the healing process.

Egg Binding

Egg binding occurs when a female is unable or unwilling to deposit her eggs in a timely fashion. If not treated promptly, death can result.

The primary symptoms of egg binding are similar to those that occur when a gravid turtle approaches parturition. Egg bound turtles may dig to create an egg chamber or attempt to escape their enclosure. However, unlike turtles who will deposit eggs normally, egg bound turtles continue to exhibit these symptoms without producing a clutch of eggs.

As long as you are expecting your turtle to lay eggs, you can easily monitor her behavior and act quickly if she experiences problems. However, if you are not anticipating a clutch, this type of problem can catch you by surprise.

Prolapse
Prolapses occur when a turtle's intestines protrude from its vent. This is an emergency situation that requires prompt treatment. Fortunately, intestinal prolapse is not terribly common among turtles.

You will need to take the animal to the veterinarian, who will attempt to re-insert the intestinal sections. Sometimes sutures will be necessary to keep the intestines in place while the muscles regain their tone.

Try to keep the exposed tissue damp, clean and protected while traveling to the vet. It is likely that this problem is very painful for the animal, so try to keep its stress level low during the process.

Quarantine
Quarantine is the practice of isolating animals to prevent them from transferring diseases between themselves.

If you have no other pet reptiles (particularly turtles), quarantine is unnecessary. However, if you already maintain other turtles (especially other box turtles) you must provide all new acquisitions with a separate enclosure.

At a minimum, quarantine all new acquisitions for 30 days. However, it is wiser still to extend the quarantine period for 60 to 90 days, to give yourself a better chance of discovering any illness present before exposing your colony to new, potentially sick, animals. Professional zoological institutions often quarantine animals for six months to a year. In fact, some zoos keep their animals in a state of perpetual quarantine.

Chapter 14: Breeding Box Turtles

Many – if not most – turtle keepers are eventually bitten by the captive breeding bug. Determined to produce a clutch of adorable hatchlings, these keepers acquire specimens of each sex and begin waiting for eggs.

This is a natural progression for keepers, and, when carried out in responsible fashion, breeding can be beneficial for the species, as captive breeding projects help alleviate pressure on wild populations.

However, irresponsible breeders often cause serious problems for the hobby.

Such breeders often set out with the explicit goal of profiting from their turtles, rather than enjoying their pets in their own right. This ensures failure for the vast majority of people that try to breed turtles for profit.

Pre-Breeding Considerations

Before you set out to breed box turtles, consider the decision carefully. Unfortunately, few keepers realize the implications of breeding their turtles before they set out to do so.

Ask yourself if you will be able to:

- Provide adequate care for a pair of adult turtles
- Provide the proper care for the female while gravid
- Afford emergency veterinary services if necessary
- Incubate the eggs in some type of incubator
- Provide housing for the hatchlings
- Provide food for the hatchlings

- Dedicate the time to caring for the hatchlings
- Find new homes for the hatchlings

If you cannot answer each of these questions affirmatively, you are not in a position to breed box turtles responsibly.

Legal Issues

Before deciding to breed turtles, you must investigate the relevant laws in your area. Some municipalities require turtle breeders to obtain licenses, insurance and permits, although others do not.

Finally, be aware that it is illegal to buy or sell turtles with carapaces less than 4 inches in length in the United States, except for educational or scientific purposes. This is a particularly important consideration when breeding relatively small turtles, because you may need to house them for some time, while waiting for them to attain the minimum size necessary.

Sexing Box Turtles

If, after considering the proposition carefully, you decide to breed box turtles, you will need at least one sexual pair of animals. To be sure that you have a sexed pair, you must be able to distinguish one sex from the other.

This can be a difficult task with some box turtles, but it is often relatively easy to distinguish between the sexes by the time they are 3 to 4 inches in length.

The best way to distinguish the sex of a box turtle is by observing the plastron; it helps if you have more than one animal, thereby allowing you to compare and contrast.

Males have concave plastrons, which allow them to mount the females, while females have flat plastrons. Additionally, male box turtles have longer, thicker tails than females do. The vent is usually positioned more distally in males than it is in females. Males often have sharply hooked, thick nails on the first toes of their rear feet.

Eye color can also provide clues to the animal's sex; males typically have red or orange eyes, while females have brown or yellow eyes.

Note that males occasionally mount other males during the breeding season. This means that an individual turtle is not necessarily a female, just because another turtle attempts to breed with it.

Pre-Breeding Conditioning

Once you have obtained a sexual pair, you must begin conditioning them for breeding. This is important because animals that are not in very good condition may not be able to handle the rigors of cycling and breeding.

Take the turtles to visit your veterinarian, who will be able to ascertain their health status. Some veterinarians may only perform a visual inspection, but others may collect biological samples for additional testing.

If your vet determines that your turtles are not healthy, take whatever steps are recommended to rectify the problem before commencing breeding trials.

Once you are certain that your turtles are in good health, it is time to initiate your breeding protocols.

Cycling

Cycling is a term used to describe the practice of providing captive reptiles with an annual variation in temperature (or other factors, such as photoperiod). The concept seeks to mimic the natural seasonal cycle and synchronize the reproductive cycle of the reptiles in question.

In some species, proper cycling appears to be necessary for successful reproduction in captivity, while other species reproduce quite successfully with no variation in temperature or any other factor.

Wild box turtles generally breed from March or April through August. However, captive box turtles may breed at any time of the year.

Groupings and Housing

Some keepers prefer to keep the sexes separate for most of the year, and only introduce them to each other during breeding trials.

One of the benefits to keeping the sexes segregated is that it often results in vigorous courting and breeding by the male. As they say, absence makes the heart grow fonder. Additionally, singular maintenance reduces the likelihood of injuries and stress for both occupants.

While keeping box turtles in separate enclosures may be ideal, few keepers can devote enough space for multiple enclosures, and males are rarely reticent to breed (in fact, the opposite problem – continued, non-stop breeding – is often the problem). Instead, most keepers maintain breeding pairs together all year long.

Many keepers maintain their box turtle in small groups. This usually works well if the enclosure is large enough and no more than one male is kept in the cage. Cohabitating males may battle viciously, which can lead to injuries, stress and domination.

It is important to use large enclosures when keeping animals in groups.

Gravid

Shortly after successful copulation, suitably healthy females become gravid. Unlike many other reptiles, turtles do not offer very many signs to indicate their reproductive condition.

Manual palpation, which is a common method for determining the reproductive condition of many other reptiles, is rarely helpful with turtles. In fact, attempting to feel a female's eggs with your fingers may cause them to rupture. Accordingly, it is wise to avoid the practice entirely. Instead, the best clues lie in the female's behavior.

Many gravid box turtles females begin eating very little food as their eggs develop and take up more space in their body cavity. They may also begin to explore their surroundings and look for a suitable place to dig their eggs.

Nevertheless, the only way to be certain that your turtle is gravid is by having your veterinarian perform an x-ray. This will not only verify that she is holding eggs, but it will allow you to know approximately how many eggs she is carrying.

Egg Deposition

As the time for egg deposition nears, the female will become increasingly restless. She may pace for long periods of time or even look for a way to escape from the enclosure.

At this point, the female is seeking out a place to dig a nest and deposit her eggs. Hopefully, you have designed the enclosure so that such a place is always available, but, if you have not, you must provide her with a place she finds suitable.

Typically, box turtles look for a warm, sunny area, with a substrate suitable for nest construction. They prefer an area of exposed dirt, rather than having to dig through grass or vegetation.

Ideally, the egg-deposition site should have a footprint of at least two to three times the size of the turtle's shell and contain substrate as deep as the turtle's shell is long.

If your female does not find the provided site to her liking, you will need to tweak it until she feels comfortable. This can mean loosening the substrate, compacting the substrate, providing a greater depth of substrate or moving the egg deposition site to another location in the enclosure.

This is often a challenging component of turtle breeding, and even highly experienced zookeepers occasionally have problems devising a suitable egg-laying site.

If your turtle cannot find a suitable place to lay her eggs, she may scatter the eggs in the enclosure or retain them internally. Usually, these outcomes lead to health problems for the female, such as dystocia (egg binding).

Assuming that your turtle finds the egg deposition area suitable, she will eventually crawl into it, dig a small depression and fill it with eggs. After completing the process, she will cover the hole and leave the area. It can be very difficult to locate a nest site afterwards, so do your best to mark the location during, or immediately after, parturition.

Egg Incubation

Keepers employ any of several different strategies for incubating box turtle eggs. No one method is "correct," although artificially incubating the eggs in a climate-controlled container usually leads to the greatest success.

The least labor-intensive approach for those housing box turtles outdoors is to leave the eggs where they are and let them incubate naturally. After all, box turtles have been incubating their eggs in just this way for millions of years.

However, doing so is unlikely to lead to a high rate of success, as you have little control over the temperatures of the mass. Additionally, the eggs may be vulnerable to predators, including rodents or fire ants.

You will need to be very observant for emerging hatchlings, which may make their way out of the nest over the course of a month or more.

If you would prefer more control of the incubation process, you can excavate the egg chamber, remove the eggs and place them in a climate-controlled incubator for the remainder of their development.

Use great care when excavating the egg chamber to prevent damaging the eggs. Once you have accessed the eggs, mark the top of each with a graphite pencil. This will allow you to maintain the correct orientation when transferring the eggs to the incubator; inverting the eggs can cause the embryos to drown.

Avoid separating any eggs that have adhered to each other. While it is often possible to do so without damaging the eggs, such attempts should be left to those who have considerable experience incubating reptile eggs.

Egg Boxes

Egg boxes are small plastic storage boxes designed to hold the eggs inside the incubator. While their use is not always necessary in the strictest sense, they make it easier to maintain the climate surrounding the eggs.

Virtually any type of small plastic storage box will suffice, but consider a few things before selecting your egg boxes:

1. Be sure to select boxes that are tall enough to contain 1 or 2 inches (2.5 to 5 centimeters) of incubation media as well as the eggs, which will rest on top of the media (partially buried).
2. Whenever possible, select transparent egg boxes so that you can observe the eggs without having to open them.
3. If possible, select boxes with domed lids, which will help prevent condensation from dripping on the eggs.

You will need to make two small holes (approximately one-quarter-inch or one-half centimeter in diameter) in each box to allow for air exchange inside the egg boxes.

Some breeders prefer to monitor the temperature of the egg boxes, while others prefer to monitor the temperature of the incubator. Either method will work, although if you desire to measure the temperatures inside the egg boxes, you will need to drill additional holes to accept a temperature probe.

You can select relatively large egg boxes so that they will accommodate large clutches, or you can use relatively small egg boxes, so that you can split up the clutch into several different sub groups.

Incubation Media

Several different incubation media are appropriate for egg incubation. Soil, soil and sand mixtures and vermiculite are some of the most common choices by breeders. Vermiculite works for a wide variety of reptile eggs, as it is quite easy to attain a suitable moisture level.

The substrate not only provides a protective cushion that supports the eggs, but it also provides moisture, which will keep the relative humidity of the egg box high. This will prevent the eggs from desiccating.

Too much humidity or dampness, however, can have a negative effect on the eggs, so it is important to keep enough water in the egg boxes, but not too much.

Many keepers strive to maintain humidity levels of 80 percent in the egg chamber, but others simply watch the eggs and adjust the humidity accordingly. If the eggs begin to exhibit wrinkles, they are drying out and more water is necessary. Conversely, if they begin to swell or exude fluid, the humidity should be lowered.

Some authorities recommend specific ratios of water and vermiculite, but as vermiculite absorbs water from the air, it is impossible to know how saturated the vermiculite was when you started.

Accordingly, the best approach is to judge the moisture with your hands. Beginning with dry vermiculite, slowly add water while stirring the mixture. The goal is to dampen the vermiculite just enough that it clumps when compressed in your hand. However, if water drips from the media when you squeeze it, the vermiculite is too damp.

The Incubator

You can either purchase a commercially produced incubator or construct your own. However, most beginning breeders are better served by purchasing a commercial incubator than making their own.

Commercial Incubators

Commercial egg incubators come in myriad styles and sizes. Some of the most popular models are similar to those used to incubate poultry eggs (these are often available for purchase from livestock supply retailers).

These incubators are constructed from a large foam box, fitted with a heating element and thermostat. Some models feature a fan for circulating air; while helpful for maintaining a uniform thermal environment, models that lack these fans are acceptable.

You can place an incubation medium directly in the bottom of these types of incubators, although it is preferable to place the media (and eggs) inside small plastic storage boxes, which are then placed inside the incubator.

These incubators are usually affordable and easy to use, although their foam-based construction makes them less durable than most premium incubators are.

Other incubators are constructed from metal or plastic boxes; feature a clear door, an enclosed heating element and a thermostat. Some units also feature a backup thermostat, which can provide some additional protection in case the primary thermostat fails.

These types of incubators usually outperform economy, foam-based models, but they also bear higher price tags. Either style will work, but, if you plan to breed turtles for many years, premium models usually present the best option.

Homemade Incubators
Although incubators can be constructed in a variety of ways, using many different materials and designs, two basic designs are most common.

The first type of homemade incubator consists of a plastic, glass or wood box, and a simple heat source, such as a piece of heat tape or a low-wattage heat lamp. The heating source must be attached to a thermostat to keep the temperatures consistent. A thermometer is also necessary for monitoring the temperatures of the incubator.

Some keepers make these types of incubators from wood, while others prefer plastic or foam. Although glass is a poor insulator, aquariums often serve as acceptable incubators; however, you must purchase or construct a solid top to retain heat.

Place a brick on the bottom of the incubator, and place the egg box on top of the brick, so that the eggs are not resting directly on the heat tape. The brick will also provide thermal mass to the incubator, which will help maintain a more consistent temperature.

The other popular incubator design adds a quantity of water to the design to help maintain consistent temperatures and a higher humidity. To build such a unit, begin with an aquarium fitted with a glass or plastic lid.

Place a brick in the bottom of the aquarium and add about two gallons of water to the aquarium; ideally, the water level should stop right below the top of the brick.

Add an aquarium heater to the water and set the thermostat to the desired temperature. Place the egg box on the brick, insert a temperature probe into the egg box and cover the aquarium with the lid (you may need to purchase a lid designed to allow the cords to pass through it).

This type of incubator works by heating the water, which will in turn heat the air inside the incubator, which will heat the eggs. Although it can take several days of repeated adjustments to get these types of incubators set to the exact temperature you would like, they are very stable once established.

Incubation Temperature and Duration

As with the adult animals, the biological processes taking place inside reptile eggs are determined by the temperature at which they are kept. The warmer the environment is, the quicker the eggs develop; the cooler the environment is, the longer it takes the eggs to complete their development.

This basic principle holds true for box turtles. However, this does not mean that their eggs can be incubated at any temperature. Eggs kept below the minimum acceptable temperature will fail to live, just as those kept above the maximum acceptable temperature.

The ideal range for box turtle egg incubation is between about 72 and 88 degrees Fahrenheit (22 to 31 degrees Celsius). Higher incubation temperatures cause the embryos to develop more quickly than those incubated at lower temperatures do.

Depending on the temperature of your home – you may be able to incubate the eggs at "room temperature."

However, doing so will invariably expose the eggs to temperature fluctuations. Minor temperature fluctuations are not harmful to the eggs, but massive swings in temperature predispose the eggs to failure or cause the young to be abnormal.

The duration of incubation varies depending on the temperature and the length of the female's gestation period. Most box turtle eggs hatch approximately 50 to 60 days after being deposited. However, individuals develop at slightly different speeds, so the young may hatch over a period of days. In some cases, the first and last hatchling to emerge from the eggs may be separated by a week's time.

Sex Determination

The sex of box turtles is determined by the temperature at which they are incubated. This phenomenon is called temperature dependent sex determination (abbreviated TSD or TDSD) and is common among many different reptile lineages, including crocodilians, geckos and many other chelonians.

This means that, in theory, you can control the temperature of the egg mass (or individual eggs) with precision, you can deliberately create male or female hatchlings.

In general, clutches incubated at 72 degrees Fahrenheit (22 degrees Celsius) become almost entirely male; while clutches incubated at 88 degrees Fahrenheit (31 degrees Celsius) become almost entirely female. Mixed clutches occur at intermediate temperatures. A 50-50 mix can be produced by incubating the clutch at about 84 degrees Fahrenheit (29 degrees Celsius).

A hatchling box turtle.

Neonatal Husbandry

Observe the hatchlings as they emerge from their shells. Some turtles will remain in their shells for several days while they absorb the rest of their egg yolk. This is perfectly normal, and you should NOT remove such turtles from their eggs. Allow the turtle to absorb the entire yolk and exit the egg on his own.

If for some reason, the egg becomes destroyed (such as through the activities of the clutchmates), move the turtle into a clean, plastic container with about 1/4 inch of water in the bottom. Do not pull the yolk free, and try to keep it from drying out.

Once the turtles have hatched and absorbed their egg yolk, they are ready to move to the nursery. The nursery container should be constructed from a small plastic storage box (you can split the clutch among several different boxes to reduce the stress on the hatchlings).

Drill or melt a few small ventilation holes in the top (always making sure the holes are drilled from the inside toward the outside to prevent any sharp edges from injuring the hatchlings) and place a few layers of paper towels on the bottom.

Add a very shallow water dish to the center of the cage (a 3-inch plant saucer works well) and keep it full of clean water. Leave the hatchlings inside the nursery for at least 24 hours to ensure they have absorbed their egg yolks are have become active.

Once a turtle has become active, you can move it to its "permanent" home. You can house a few hatchlings together in the same habitat, but avoid overcrowding them, which can lead to squabbles and injuries. Be sure there are more places to hide than there are turtles in the tank.

You can begin feeding them almost immediately after placing them in their new homes, but many will not begin feeding for a few days.

Chapter 15: Unusual Box Turtles

Although box turtles are quite variable, but this variation occurs within a "typical range." Most box turtles are primarily clad in earth tones, although some have bright orange or yellow markings. However, every once in a while, a genetic mutation pops up that gives rise to animals whose unusual looks far surpass what can be explained by normal individual variation.

For example, box turtles that fail to produce melanin are occasionally found, as are those that produce less melanin than normal. These animals are often brightly colored, and referred to as albino or hypomelanistic animals, respectively.

Because of the way in which these mutations are passed from parent to offspring, these spectacular animals remain relatively rare, even among captive populations.

Common Mutations

In contrast to some other common reptile pets, such as ball pythons (*Python regius*) and leopard geckos (*Eublepharis macularius*), for which many color mutations have been discovered, only a handful of color mutations have been documented in box turtles.

Sometimes, the distinction between an animal harboring a genetic mutation and one that simply looks different because of individual variation is difficult to determine. Ultimately, breeding trials are necessary to determine whether the trait is a heritable condition.

At the time of this publication, several different box turtles color mutations have been documented, but none are common in the captive gene pool. However, overtime, these mutants are likely to become more common.

Patterns of Inheritance

Turtles receive one copy of each gene from their mother and one from their father. Some genes affect the animal's appearance when only one copy is present, while others require two copies of a gene to express the associated trait.

Animals with two copies of the same gene are said to be homozygous. Conversely, animals with one copy of a mutant gene and one copy of the normal gene are called heterozygous.

Simple Recessive

Simple recessive traits are only expressed when an animal has two copies of the mutant gene. However, normal looking, but heterozygous animals may produce offspring that display the trait associated with the gene, if the other parent has a copy of the gene as well.

Dominant

Dominant traits are expressed whenever they are present, regardless of the other gene in the pair. Accordingly, dominant traits become very common in a given gene pool. For example, the genes associated with the normal appearance of box turtles are dominant over most genes.

There is no visual difference between an animal with one copy of a dominant gene or two copies of the gene. However, animals that are homozygous for the dominant trait only produce young that express the dominant gene.

Incompletely Dominant

Incompletely dominant mutations are similar to dominant mutations except that those with one copy of the gene look different from those with two copies of the mutant gene.

Often, heterozygous animals display a trait (such as some forms of hypomelanism), while homozygous animals display a more extreme version of the trait (such as the so-called "super hypomelanistic" animals).

Often, incompletely dominant mutations are called co-dominant mutations. However, this terminology is not technically correct, as animals that display co-dominant traits possess more than one mutant gene.

Polygenetic Traits

Some physical traits of box turtles are determined by the complicated interactions of several different genes. Size potential and growth rate, for example, are likely controlled by a collection of genes.

Polygenetic traits are not inherited in a predictable fashion. However, they can often be refined through selective breeding efforts.

Genetic Traits and Marketing

Unusual specimens often command very high prices, which can make turtle breeding a profitable endeavor in some cases. While there is nothing inherently wrong with this fact, the prospect of high profits often leads keepers to experience problems.

While some of these problems are born of honest mistakes or misunderstandings, others are the result of outright fraud.

To avoid these problems, those who hatch unusual looking turtles should attempt to reproduce the mutation before labelling it as a genetically inheritable condition. However, in an effort to get the animals to market quickly, some breeders market the animals in deceptive ways.

Accordingly, it is always wise to do your homework before deciding to purchase a box turtle with a rare color mutation. Additionally, it is wise to avoid purchasing turtles from shady, disreputable or evasive breeders, particularly if they are making extraordinary claims about their animals.

Chapter 16: Notes on a Few Species and Subspecies

Four different box turtle species or subspecies are of special interest. Three of the forms are the most common in captivity, while the other species is rather rare in captivity, but particularly noteworthy.

Eastern Box Turtle (*Terrapene carolina carolina*)

Eastern box turtles are probably the most commonly kept of the various box turtle species and subspecies, and they are likely the form that adapts best to captivity.

Eastern box turtles are some of the most variable box turtles, and even siblings often look quite different from each other. Some eastern box turtles are quite attractive and clad in bright yellow and orange tones. Others display more muted earth tones, with only a hint of yellow or orange markings.

Eastern box turtles are typically forest-dwelling turtles, who benefit from higher humidity levels than ornate turtles do. However, this is not to suggest that they thrive in permanently damp, humid enclosures. It is important to provide them with moderate humidity levels, while offering them a damp retreat in which they will spend a large part of their time.

Like their western counterparts, eastern box turtles consume a wide variety of invertebrates and small vertebrates, but they also consume an array of plant-based foods.

In fact, eastern box turtles consume more fruits and vegetables than most other species and subspecies, so be sure to include plenty of plant-based materials in their diet.

Note the red eyes on this male eastern box turtle.

Ornate Box Turtles (*Terrapene ornata ornata*)

Ornate box turtles are another commonly kept box turtle species. Ornate box turtles are among the smaller variety of box turtle and they feature a slightly different shell shape than most other forms. Instead of a highly domed shell, the top of an ornate box turtle's shell is usually flattened.

Ornate box turtles are most often clad in dark earth tones, with a pattern of radiating orange or yellow lines or spots on each scute.

Hailing from drier habitats than eastern box turtles, ornate box turtles prefer slightly drier conditions than forest-dwelling turtles do. However, they are still susceptible to dehydration, so it is imperative to offer ornate box turtles a damp retreat in which they can hide.

Ornate box turtles typically prefer insects and other invertebrates to other types of foods, but it is still important to provide them with plant-based foods to ensure they receive a balanced diet.

A unique-looking ornate box turtle.

Three-Toed Box Turtle (*Ter rapene carolina triunguis*)

Named for the regularity with which these turtles display only three toes on their rear legs, three-toed box turtles are another common form found in captive collections. However, many three-toed box turtles possess four toes on their rear legs, so you cannot always identify the species by counting its toes. Some workers believe that four-toed individuals are actually intergrades between three-toed and eastern box turtles, but the truth remains unclear.

A member of the eastern box turtle species, this subspecies is found to the southeast of the primary eastern box turtle range.

A three-toed box turtle.

Three toed box turtles often display fewer markings than eastern box turtles do, and they tend toward an unmarked appearance. Their shells also bear a slightly different shape than their eastern cousins, as the highest part of the carapace is located further back (posteriorly) than it is in eastern box turtles.

Three-toed box turtles are otherwise similar to the eastern subspecies, in terms of husbandry and behavior. They require a moderately high humidity, and access to damp retreats.

The Coahuilan Box Turtle (*Terrapene coahuila*)

The Coahuilan box turtle is not nearly as common among captive collections as the preveious three mentioned forms. However, this is slowly beginning to change, and a larger number of these turtles are appearing in the marketplace.

Coahuilan box turtles are very different from other box turtle species, despite their close evolutionary relationship. While most box turtles will take advantage of shallow water bodies, and spend some time foraging or soaking in the water, Coahuilan box turtles spend most of their time in shallow streams, wetlands and other aquatic habitats.

Coahuilan box turtles subsist on standard box turtle fare, including insects, minnows, berries and earthworms.

The Coahuilan box turtle.

Supplemental Information

Never stop learning more about your new pet's natural history, biology and captive care. Doing so will help you provide your new pet with the highest quality of life possible.

Further Reading

Bookstores and online book retailers often offer a treasure trove of information that will advance your quest for knowledge. While books represent an additional cost involved in reptile care, you can consider it an investment in your pet's well-being. Your local library may also carry some books about turtles, which you can borrow for no charge.

University libraries are a great place for finding old, obscure or academically oriented books about turtles. You may not be allowed to borrow these books if you are not a student, but you can view and read them at the library.

Herpetology: An Introductory Biology of Amphibians and Reptiles

By Laurie J. Vitt, Janalee P. Caldwell

Academic Press, 2013

Understanding Reptile Parasites: A Basic Manual for Herpetoculturists & Veterinarians

By Roger Klingenberg D.V.M.

Advanced Vivarium Systems, 1997

Infectious Diseases and Pathology of Reptiles: Color Atlas and Text

Elliott Jacobson

CRC Press

Designer Reptiles and Amphibians

Richard D. Bartlett, Patricia Bartlett

Barron's Educational Series

Magazines

Like books, magazines can offer an abundance of information. Additionally, because they are typically published several times each year, they often provide more current information than books do.

Reptiles Magazine

www.reptilesmagazine.com/

This publication covers all facets of reptile husbandry, breeding and care.

Practical Reptile Keeping

http://www.practicalreptilekeeping.co.uk/

Practical Reptile Keeping is a popular publication aimed at beginning and advanced hobbies. Topics include the care and maintenance of popular reptiles as well as information on wild reptiles.

Websites

With the explosion of the internet, it is easier to find information about reptiles than it has ever been. However, this growth has cause an increase in the proliferation of both good information and bad information.

While knowledgeable breeders, keepers and academics operate some websites, other webmasters lack the same dedication and scientific rigor. Anyone with a computer and internet connection can launch a website and say virtually anything they want about turtles. Accordingly, as with all other research, consider the source of the information before making any husbandry decisions.

The Reptile Report

www.thereptilereport.com/

The Reptile Report is a news-aggregating website that accumulates interesting stories and features about reptiles from around the world.

Kingsnake.com

www.kingsnake.com

Started as a small website for gray-banded kingsnake enthusiasts, Kingsnake.com has become one of the largest reptile-oriented portals in the hobby. Includes classifieds, breeder directories, message forums and other resources.

The Vivarium and Aquarium News

www.vivariumnews.com/

The online version of the former publication, The Vivarium and Aquarium News provides in-depth coverage of different reptiles and amphibians in a captive and wild context.

Journals

Journals are the primary place professional scientists turn when they need to learn about turtles. While they may not make light reading, hobbyists stand to learn a great deal from journals.

Herpetologica

www.hljournals.org/

Published by The Herpetologists' League, Herpetologica, and its companion publication, Herpetological Monographs cover all aspects of reptile and amphibian research.

Journal of Herpetology

www.ssarherps.org/

Produced by the Society for the Study of Reptiles and Amphibians, the Journal of Herpetology is a peer-reviewed publication covering a variety of reptile-related topics.

Copeia

www.asihcopeiaonline.org/

Copeia is published by the American Society of Ichthyologists and Herpetologists. A peer-reviewed journal, Copeia covers all aspects of the biology of reptiles, amphibians and fish.

Nature

www.nature.com/

Although Nature covers all aspects of the natural world, there is plenty to appeal to turtle enthusiasts.

Supplies

While you can obtain some of the supplies you need from local pet stores, home improvement stores and grocery stores, you may need to search widely to find some supplies and tools. Some of the following retailers sell a variety of husbandry tools and supplies.

Big Apple Pet Supply

http://www.bigappleherp.com

Big Apple Pet Supply carries most common husbandry equipment, including heating devices, water dishes and substrates.

LLLReptile

http://www.lllreptile.com

LLL Reptile carries a wide variety of husbandry tools, heating devices, lighting products and more.

Doctors Foster and Smith

http://www.drsfostersmith.com

Foster and Smith is a veterinarian-owned retailer that supplies husbandry-related items to pet keepers.

Support Organizations

Sometimes, the best way to learn about turtles is to reach out to other keepers and breeders. Check out these organizations, and search for others in your geographic area.

The National Reptile & Amphibian Advisory Council

http://www.nraac.org/

The National Reptile & Amphibian Advisory Council seeks to educate the hobbyists, legislators and the public about reptile and amphibian related issues.

American Veterinary Medical Association

www.avma.org

The AVMA is a good place for Americans to turn if you are having trouble finding a suitable reptile veterinarian.

The World Veterinary Association

http://www.worldvet.org/

The World Veterinary Association is a good resource for finding suitable reptile veterinarians worldwide.

References

Anderson, S. P. (2003). The Phylogenetic Definition of Reptilia. *Systematic Biology*.

Crawford, N. G. (2012). A phylogenomic analysis of turtles. *Molecular Phylogenetics and Evolution*.

Gist, L. R. (1975). Seminal Receptacles in the Eastern Box Turtle, Terrapene carolina. *Copeia*.

Joanne Braun and Garnett R. Brooks, J. (1987). Box Turtles (Terrapene carolina) as Potential Agents for Seed Dispersal. *The American Midland Naturalist*.

Miller, J. (2001). Escaping Senescence: Demographic Data from the Three-Toed Box Turtle (Terrapene carolina triunguis). *Experimental Gerontology*.

Stickel, L. F. (1989). Home Range Behavior among Box Turtles (Terrapene c. carolina) of a Bottomland Forest in. *Journal of Herpetology*.

Strang, C. A. (1983). Spatial and Temporal Activity Patterns in Two Terrestrial Turtles. *Journal of Herpetology*.

Wallace B Baze, F. R. (1970). Ureogenesis in chelonia. *Comparative Biochemistry and Physiology*.

William R. Belzer, S. S. (2000). Putative Chipmunk Predation of Juvenile Eastern Box Turtles. *Turtle and Tortoise Newsletter*.

Index

131

www.ingramcontent.com/pod-product-compliance
Lightning Source LLC
LaVergne TN
LVHW050625090426
835512LV00007B/665